fabric to dye for

30 fabulous projects to
make using dip-dyed,
tie-dyed, space-dyed
and marbled fabric

susie stokoe

southwater

This edition is published by Southwater

Southwater is an imprint of Anness Publishing Ltd
Hermes House, 88–89 Blackfriars Road, London SE1 8HA
tel. 020 7401 2077; fax 020 7633 9499
www.southwaterbooks.com; info@anness.com

© Anness Publishing Ltd 2002

Published in the USA by Southwater,
Anness Publishing Inc.
27 West 20th Street,
New York, NY 10011;
fax 212 807 6813

This edition distributed in the UK by
The Manning Partnership
251–253 London Road East,
Batheaston, Bath BA1 7RL
tel. 01225 852 727;
fax 01225 852 852;
sales@manning-partnership.co.uk

This edition distributed in the USA
by National Book Network
4720 Boston Way,
Lanham, MD 20706
tel. 301 459 3366;
fax 301 459 1705;
www.nbnbooks.com

This edition distributed in Canada
by General Publishing
895 Don Mills Road,
400–402 Park Centre,
Toronto, Ontario M3C 1W3
tel. 416 445 3333;
fax 416 445 5991;
www.genpub.com

This edition distributed in Australia
by Pan Macmillan Australia
Level 18, St Martins Tower
31 Market St, Sydney, NSW 2000
tel. 1300 135 113;
fax 1300 135 103; email
customer.service@macmillan.com.au

This edition distributed in New Zealand by
The Five Mile Press (NZ) Ltd
PO Box 33-1071 Takapuna,
Unit 11/101-111 Diana Drive,
Glenfield, Auckland 10
tel. (09) 444 4144;
fax (09) 444 4518;
fivemilenz@clear.net.nz

A CIP catalogue record for this book is available from the British Library.

Publisher: Joanna Lorenz
Managing Editor: Helen Sudell
Project Editor: Simona Hill
Designer: Jane Coney
Production Controller: Claire Rae

Previously published as part of a larger compendium, *Decorating Fabric*

10 9 8 7 6 5 4 3 2 1

A few basic safety rules should be followed when working with dyes. Label all
solutions and keep them away from children and animals. Do not eat or drink
while using dyes, and wash your hands before handling food. If you spill dye
powder, sweep up as much as possible before washing with plenty of water.
Blot up spilt dye solution with newspaper, then wash down. Remove dye stains
from hard surfaces with household cleaner or diluted bleach.

acknowledgements

The publishers would like to thank the following
people for designing projects in this book:
Penny Boylan for the Velvet-edged Throw p20–21
and Tea-dyed Hot Water Bottle Cover p28–29.
Stephanie Donaldson for the Mermaid Shower
Curtain p17.
Lucinda Ganderton for the Marbled Spectacle Case
p24–25 and Tie-dyed Jewellery Roll p38–39.
Judith Gussin for the Crazy Patchwork Cushion
p70–71, Spray-dyed Lavender Bags p72–73, Dye-
painted Cosmetic Bag p76–77, Party Tablecloth
p78–79, Patchwork Toy Bag p80–81, Teddy Bear Rug
p82–84, Paisley Pelmet p85–87, Quilted Wallhanging
p88–91 and Indian Birds p92–93.
Sheila Gussin for the Delicate Muslin Curtain p68–69,
Embroidered Pincushion p74–75, and for designing
the Teddy Bear Rug p82–84.
Karin Hossack for the Doughnut Floor Cushion
p44–45.
Alison Jenkins for the Marbled Fabric Desk Set
p36–37 and Folded Napkin Parcels p50–51.
Isabel Stanley for the Marbled Book Cover p54–55.
Susie Stokoe for the Dip-dyed Lampshade p18–19,
Double-dyed Place Mats p30–31, Folded Silk
Handkerchiefs p32–33, Pleated Table Runner p34–35,
Tassel-edged Lampshade p40–41, Velvet Blind p42–43,
Tie-dyed Duvet Cover p46–47, Tie-dyed Patchwork
Cushion p48–49 and Tie-dyed Patchwork Bedspread
52–53.

fabric to dye for

contents

Introduction   6

Dyeing and Marbling   **8**
Colour Control   10
Materials and Equipment   12
Techniques   14
Mermaid Shower Curtain   17
Dip-dyed Lampshade   18
Velvet-edged Throw   20
Marbled Drawstring Bag   22
Marbled Spectacle Case   24
Marbled Headband   26
Tea-dyed Hot Water Bottle Cover   28
Double-dyed Place Mats   30
Folded Silk Handkerchiefs   32
Pleated Table Runner   34
Marbled Fabric Desk Set   36
Tie-dyed Jewellery Roll   38
Tassel-edged Lampshade   40
Velvet Blind   42
Doughnut Floor Cushion   44
Tie-dyed Duvet Cover   46
Tie-dyed Patchwork Cushion   48
Folded Napkin Parcels   50
Tie-dyed Patchwork Bedspread   52
Marbled Book Cover   54

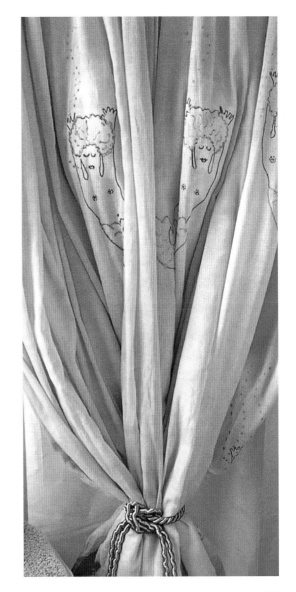

Space-dyeing   **56**
Random Reactions   58
Materials and Equipment   60
Techniques   62
Delicate Muslin Curtain   68
Crazy Patchwork Cushion   70
Spray-dyed Lavender Bags   72
Embroidered Pincushion   74
Dye-painted Cosmetic Bag   76
Party Tablecloth   78
Patchwork Toy Bag   80
Teddy Bear Rug   82
Paisley Pelmet   85
Quilted Wallhanging   88
Indian Birds   92

Templates   94
Index   96

Introduction

Dyeing is one of the easiest ways of changing the colour of fabric. Although less controlled than applying colour with a brush, dyeing fabric in a dye bath can produce a variety of effects. This book is all about having fun with colour.

At its simplest, dyeing fabric involves immersing a piece of fabric in a dye bath of either hot or cold dye, leaving it for the recommended time, and fixing it. But there is a lot more to dyeing than simple immersion. Try dipping the edges of fabric into the dye bath to create a band of colour, or mixing several dye colours together to create your

own fabulous blend. You can bind the fabric with string before immersing it in dye to create circular or striped tie-dyed patterns, or you can decorate the fabric with marbled patterns by swirling patches of dye in a dye bath, then laying

the fabric over the top to "pick up" the pattern.

Space-dyeing is another more unusual method of dyeing which is less controllable than dip-dyeing. The aim is to create a random multi-coloured pattern using several different colours at once and

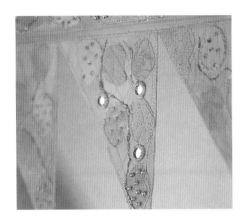

crumpling the fabric so that the dye is not absorbed evenly. You can also apply the dye with a brush, sprayer or sprinkler, rather than putting the fabric in a dye bath.

All the materials and equipment for each dyeing technique are listed at the beginning of each chapter, while the basic techniques are explained and illustrated with step-by-step photographs. Once you are confident of these techniques, have a go at some of the dyeing projects featured. (The easy

projects have a single brush above the list of materials, while a difficult project is denoted by five brushes.) Try decorating a lampshade, curtains or

duvet cover, or make a spectacle case or drawstring bag using marbled fabric. Decorate your dining room furnishings by dyeing a tablecloth, place mats, napkins and a table runner, or add zest to your living room with dyed patchwork cushions, a velvet blind, a felt rug and a quilted wallhanging. Whatever you choose, this book contains plenty of projects to inspire you.

Dyeing and Marbling

There are many ways of dyeing fabric – some methods can be used to create fairly controlled patterns, though not usually as detailed or specific as fabric painting or printing, while other techniques produce much more random effects. This unpredictability is a big part of the appeal of dyeing, opening up a wide range of creative possibilities for the dyed fabric and making each piece unique.

Colour Control

The wide range of dyes available for both hot and cold dyeing makes this method of colouring fabric as simple as it is stimulating.

In dip-dyeing, the art is often to blend colours so that they bleed together, creating a lovely feathery effect. You can also fold a napkin or handkerchief, then dip it into the dye so that just the tips of the folded edges take up the colour. Dip-dyeing is also very practical for dyeing awkward objects such as a lampshade, or items too large to be immersed in a dye bath.

Tie-dyeing works by preventing the dye from penetrating certain areas of the fabric. Horizontal stripes are achieved by folding or pleating the fabric; the pleats are then bound tightly with string or cord. Circular designs are made by tying round objects such as buttons,

coins or lentils into the fabric, using string, cord or rubber bands. Experiment with different binding materials, as these contribute to the finished design. When the bindings and tied objects are removed after dyeing, these areas show up as plain

undyed fabric. Tie-dyeing works well on rich fabrics such as velvet and silk, or you can create striking modern effects using cotton fabrics dyed in a single bold colour. The size of each piece of tie-dyed fabric is limited to the size of the dye bath, but to make larger projects you can stitch pieces together using the patchwork technique.

Marbled fabric uses the same technique as marbled paper. Circles of marbling dye are dropped on to the surface of a shallow dye bath, then gently dragged into decorative patterns. Again, the size of each piece of marbled fabric is limited to the size of the dye bath, so this lovely traditional fabric is

often used, like marbled paper, to cover desk sets and book covers.

Various resist mediums can be applied to fabric before dyeing. These are available in applicators with a nozzle, which makes drawing or tracing a detailed design simple. Finally, one of the most readily available of all dyes is tea, which can be brewed to any strength to give warm pale brown tones.

The most important materials used in this chapter are the dyes. Household dyes, suitable for most fabrics, are widely available. Special dye kits, including a thickening medium, are available for marbling.

Materials

dry. Remember to take the colour of the original fabric into account if you are dyeing a coloured fabric. Pre-wash fabrics to remove any dressing.

Marbling thickening medium

This solution is added to the water in the dye bath before adding marbling dyes. Carefully follow the manufacturer's instructions.

Paper

Use stiff white paper to make patchwork templates, remembering that you need to hand stitch through the paper as well as the fabric. You can also clean the marbling dyes from the dye bath with newspaper layers.

Resist medium

Painted on to areas of fabric to prevent them taking up the dye.

Absorbent cloth or paper

Use for resting dyed fabrics on to dry.

Dyes

Available in powder or liquid form. Hot-water dyes provide better colour penetration into the fibres, but may shrink the fabric, so cold-water dyes are preferable for some fabrics, such as wool and silk. Always follow the dye manufacturer's instructions. Special water-based dyes are available for marbling effects.

Fabric etching medium

Use to remove the pile from fabrics such as velvet. Available in a bottle with a nozzle for drawing designs.

Fabrics

Tie-dyeing works well on luxury fabrics such as velvet and silk, as well as on cotton fabrics. Lightweight fabrics without texture, such as fine silk or cotton, are most suitable for marbling. Unwieldy fabrics such as fake fur can be dip-dyed, then hung outdoors to

Rubber bands

Use to bind circular tie-dyed objects, to form a barrier to the dye.

Salt

Often added to a dye bath to fix (set) the dyes. Follow the dye manufacturer's instructions.

String and cord

Use to tightly bind tie-dyed objects. Experiment with various thicknesses to create different effects.

The essential piece of equipment is a dye bath. Use a bath large enough and deep enough to immerse the fabric completely so that it is evenly dyed. Work outdoors if possible.

Equipment

Masking tape

Use to attach fabric or a design temporarily to the work surface.

Measuring jug (cup)

Use to mix dyes and marbling thickening medium before adding them to a dye bath.

Measuring spoon

Used to measure powder dyes.

Needle

Use an ordinary sewing needle for hand stitching, and an embroidery needle for embroidery thread (floss).

Paintbrush

Use a fine artist's paintbrush to drop marbling dyes on to the surface of the dye bath solution.

Pipette (eye dropper)

Use to drop marbling dyes on to the surface of the dye bath solution.

Rubber gloves

Wear rubber gloves to avoid staining your hands.

Set square (t-square)

Useful for checking accurate squares.

Vanishing fabric marker

Use to draw temporary designs on to fabric, or use tailor's chalk.

Cocktail stick (toothpick)

Use to pull or drag circles of marbling dye into patterns. A wooden cocktail stick (toothpick) is most suitable.

Comb

Use to create feathery marbling patterns. Make a marbling comb by taping pins to a piece of dowel.

Dye baths

Use plastic bowls or a cat litter tray for cold-water dyeing, and a heatproof metal bowl or an old saucepan for hot-water dyeing. The bath must be large enough for the fabric to be immersed completely and as flat as possible. A large, shallow dye bath is used for marbling.

Iron

Use to press pleats into fabric before tie-dyeing. Also use an iron to press the finished dyed fabric and to fix (set) the dyes, following the dye manufacturer's instructions.

The dyeing techniques used in this chapter are all very simple to do. If you are dyeing a coloured fabric, consider how the colours will blend to create the final result.

Techniques

Making up a dye solution

Household dyes are sold in tablet form. These dyes penetrate the fibres of natural fabrics such as cotton, silk, wool and linen easily.

1 Dissolve the tablet or powder dye in the specified amount of water. Stir, then add to the dye bath.

2 Add the fabric. The dye bath should be large enough for the fabric to move freely.

3 Tea dyeing dyes fabric so that it has an antique cream colour. Place a tea bag in water until the required shade has been achieved.

Dip-dyeing

This technique is very useful if you want to dye an object such as a fabric lampshade that cannot be immersed in a dye bath. You can also use it to dye areas of fabric with more than one colour.

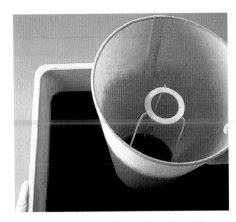

1 If you want to keep the dye colours separate, leave the fabric to dry after dipping it in the first colour and leave a small space between each colour so that the dyes cannot run together.

2 Alternatively, an attractive feathery effect can be created by dipping dip-dyed fabric into another colour while it is still slightly damp so that the two colours bleed into each other.

3 For a very simple but dramatic effect, dip just the edges of tassels or folded fabric briefly into the dye.

Tie-dyeing The charm of this technique is its unpredictability. A great variety of designs can be achieved by folding, pleating or tying objects into the fabric so that these areas resist the colour when it is immersed in a dye bath. Experiment with scraps of fabric before embarking on a project.

To make a circular design, tie round objects such as coins, buttons or lentils into the fabric before dyeing. Bind them tightly with cord, string or rubber bands so that none of the dye can leak underneath.

To create horizontal lines, fold or pleat the fabric evenly or unevenly accordion-fashion, then bind it tightly at regular intervals.

For a lacy, speckled effect, roll the fabric round a piece of string. Pull the ends of the string round to form a loop, then slide the fabric away from the ends to make a tightly gathered circle. Tie the string ends securely.

For a spider's web effect, bind a flat circular object in the fabric, then wrap string tightly around the fabric bundle. Wearing rubber gloves, prepare the dye bath using a hand dye and following the manufacturer's instructions. Use a container big enough for the fabric to be kept moving in order to achieve an even colour. Immerse the prepared fabric and move it around to ensure the dye can penetrate all areas.

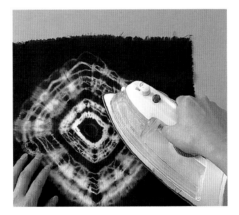

When the desired colour has been achieved (it will become more intense the longer the fabric is in the dye), remove the fabric and rinse in cold water until the water runs clear. Remove the bindings, then wash the fabric in warm water with a mild detergent. Iron flat while still damp, following the dye manufacturer's instructions, to fix (set) the dye.

Marbling

Marbling fabric is similar to marbling on paper. Lightweight and untextured fabrics such as fine silk or lightweight cotton are most suitable as they quickly and evenly absorb the dye. Special marbling dyes and dye kits are available.

1 Use a dye bath deep enough for the dye solution to be at least 4–5cm/1½–2in deep, and large enough to arrange the fabric flat. Using a measuring jug (cup), mix the marbling thickening medium then pour it into the dye bath.

2 Using a fine artist's paintbrush or pipette (eye dropper), drop the marbling dyes on to the surface of the water. The colours will spread and float on the surface. If too much dye is used, it will sink to the bottom of the dye bath and "muddy" the solution.

3 When the surface of the dye bath is covered with colour, gently tease the surface with a fine tool such as a wooden cocktail stick (toothpick) or skewer. For a feathery texture, drag a comb lightly over the surface. Make patterns by dropping dyes of different colours on top of each other, creating large ringed circles.

4 When a pleasing pattern has been arrived at, carefully place the fabric on to the inked surface. Place either the top edge or the centre of the fabric on the surface first to prevent air bubbles from forming. When the fabric has soaked up the dye, peel it away and rinse under cool water. Leave to dry before ironing.

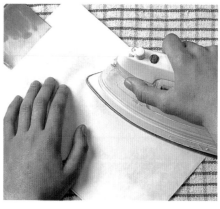

5 Fix (set) the dyes, following the manufacturer's instructions. This usually involves ironing the fabric on the reverse side.

In this lovely design, the mermaids' bodies are painted with a resist medium to stop them taking up the dye, and then outlined in gold. Use cold hand dyes to give a random "watery" effect.

Mermaid Shower Curtain

you will need

scissors

8m/8yd muslin (cheesecloth)

fabric marker pen

medium artist's paintbrush

resist medium

cloth or towel

iron

sea-green cold-water dye and dye bath

gold contour-lining fabric paint

dressmaker's pins

shower curtain liner

sewing machine

matching thread

2m/2yd net curtain heading tape

2m/2yd Velcro tape

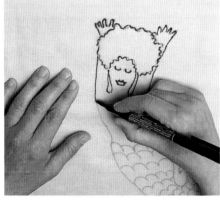

1 Cut the muslin (cheesecloth) into four pieces each 2m/2yd long and mark the position of the mermaids. Enlarge the mermaid template at the back of the book. Place each piece of muslin over the photocopy and use the fabric marker pen to draw the outline of the mermaids on to the fabric.

2 Paint the whole area of the upper body of each mermaid with resist medium. Leave to dry. Press under a cloth or towel with a hot iron for 2 minutes, to fix (set) the medium. Fold the fabric and hand dye it sea green, following the manufacturer's instructions. Iron the fabric when dry.

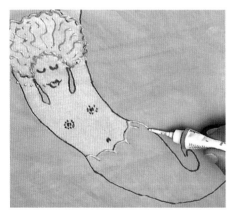

3 Paint in the hair and scales of the mermaid in gold contour paint, and add bubbles. Leave to dry flat. Pin the muslin panels together and make up to the same size as the shower curtain liner. Gather the fabric tightly on to net curtain heading tape. Attach the curtain to the liner with Velcro tape.

Dye a plain fabric lampshade in two rich colours, terracotta and cherry red, to create a lovely feathered effect. The beaded trim around the bottom is a perfect finishing touch.

Dip-dyed Lampshade

you will need
deep dye bath
cold water dyes, in cherry red
and terracotta
rubber gloves
white linen lampshade
absorbent cloths
paper and pencil
protractor
ruler
cherry red stranded embroidery
thread (floss)
large-eyed embroidery needle
12 large red glass beads
12 small beads (optional)
scissors

1 Using a deep dye bath, mix up the cherry red dye. Wearing rubber gloves, hold the lampshade by the base and dip it in the dye so that two-thirds of it is submerged. After a few seconds remove the lampshade. Repeat the process to intensify the colour. Stand the lampshade on an absorbent cloth.

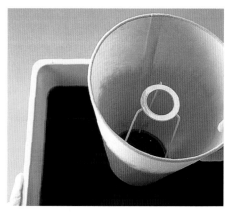

2 While the lampshade is still slightly damp, dip the top 5cm/2in in a dye bath containing terracotta dye. Stand the lampshade on an absorbent cloth to dry, allowing the second colour to bleed through the first.

3 Stand the dry lampshade upright on a piece of paper and draw around its base with a pencil. Using a protractor and ruler, divide the circle into 30° sections.

4 Stand the lampshade back on the circle, and very lightly mark the 30° sections on the bottom of the shade with the pencil.

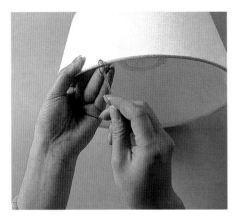

5 Double a piece of embroidery thread (floss) and thread the loop through a needle. Push this through one of the marks on the lampshade. Take the needle through the thread loop and pull tight. Thread on a large bead and tie a knot 3cm/1¼in from the base of the shade. If the knot is too small and the bead slips, thread on a small bead before knotting.

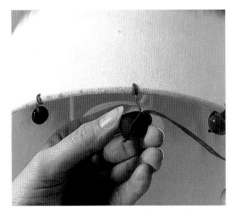

6 Take the needle back up through the large bead to hide any untidy ends, then neatly cut the thread. Following the pencil marks, repeat steps 5 and 6 until you have decorated the bottom edge of the lampshade.

If you have a store of warm, wool blankets you no longer use on the bed, colour one softly using dye to create a beautiful throw with a luxurious velvet ribbon trim.

Velvet-edged Throw

you will need

thick wool fabric

scissors

rubber gloves

hand dye

large dye bath

iron and pressing cloth

satin bias binding

sewing machine

matching sewing thread

needle

tacking (basting) thread

ruffled ribbon

wide velvet ribbon

pins

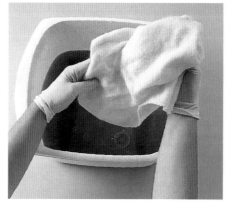

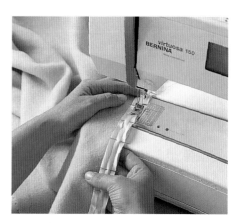

1 Trim the fabric to a square or rectangular shape and wash to remove any dressing. Make up the dye in a large dye bath and check the colour on a sample piece (which you can take with you when choosing ribbons for the edging). After dyeing, rinse the fabric very thoroughly and press under a damp cloth when dry.

2 To bind the edges, machine stitch satin bias binding to the right side all round the edge. Fold the binding over to the wrong side, and baste in place. Either machine or hand stitch in place on the wrong side to finish, folding in the excess neatly at the corners.

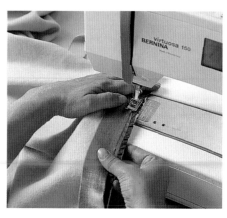

3 On the right side, stitch a length of ruffled ribbon close to the edge of the binding to cover it. Stitch along both long edges of the ribbon using matching thread.

4 Cut four lengths of velvet ribbon to fit the edges of the throw. Join the lengths by stitching diagonally across each corner, with right sides together, to create mitres.

5 Pin the ribbon carefully to the throw and stitch down on each side by hand or machine. Take care when pinning velvet as it can mark easily.

This pretty little crêpe de chine bag could be used to hold cosmetics or jewellery. If this is one of your first marbling projects, dye several pieces of fabric and choose the best.

Marbled Drawstring Bag

you will need

scissors

0.25m/¼yd silk crêpe de chine

large shallow dye bath

marbling thickening medium

rubber gloves

marbling dyes, in red, yellow and green

needle or toothpick

iron

0.25m/¼yd fine cotton, for the lining

dressmaker's pins

sewing machine

matching sewing thread

ribbon or cord

1 Cut the crêpe de chine into pieces 25 x 15cm/10 x 6in. Fill the bath with 3–5cm/1–2in of water and add the marbling thickening medium. Wearing rubber gloves, drop a little of each dye on to the surface. The colours will spread out and run into each other to cover the surface.

2 Using a needle or toothpick, make swirls and spirals. Be careful not to overmix the colours.

3 Place a piece of fabric carefully on to the marbled surface, allowing one end to touch the surface first.

4 Peel the fabric away from the surface. Rinse gently in cold water to remove the thickening medium, then dry flat. Repeat with the other pieces of fabric. Iron on the back to fix (set) the dyes. Choose the best two pieces for the outer bag and discard the rest.

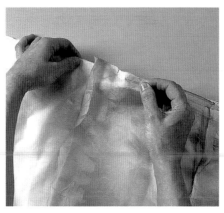

5 Cut two pieces of lining 25 x 15cm/ 10 x 6in to match the size of the marbled fabric. Place one piece of lining and one piece of marbled fabric wrong sides together and pin. Repeat. On one end of each piece of marbled fabric, fold over 5cm/2in and pin.

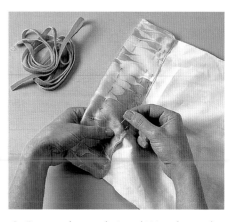

6 Pin a channel 4cm/1½in from the fold and machine stitch. With marbled sides together, machine stitch the sides and bottom of the bag, leaving the channel open. Turn right side out and thread ribbon or cord through the channel.

Quilt a piece of marbled silk fabric so that it will hold a pair of spectacles safely. Decorate the diagonal quilting pattern with small rocaille beads, and finish with ribbon roses around the top.

Marbled Spectacle Case

you will need

shallow dye bath 30cm/12in square

marbling thickening medium

fine artist's paintbrush

marbling dyes

wooden cocktail stick (toothpick)

ruler

scissors

silk, pre-washed

iron

wadding (batting)

cotton lining

needle

tacking (basting) thread

vanishing fabric marker

sewing machine

matching sewing thread

dressmaker's pins

narrow ribbon

5mm/¼in rocaille beads

6 ribbon roses

1 Prepare a shallow dye bath and add the marbling thickening medium. Scatter drops of dye on to the surface. Drag a toothpick through the dyes at intervals, first horizontally then vertically, to create a feathery pattern.

2 Cut a piece of silk 30cm/12 square to fit the dye bath. Gently place it over the marbled surface, positioning the top end or centre of the fabric on first to prevent air bubbles from becoming trapped underneath.

3 When the silk has soaked up the dye, carefully peel it away and rinse under cool water to remove the thickening medium. Leave the silk to dry, then press with a warm, dry iron to fix (set) the dyes, following the manufacturer's instructions.

4 Cut the wadding (batting) 30cm/12in square, and the lining slightly larger. Place the lining on the work surface, centre the wadding on top, then the silk. Tack (baste) the layers together, in rows 3cm/1¼in apart. Using a vanishing fabric marker, draw a diagonal grid across the surface with the lines 2.5cm/1in apart.

5 Machine stitch along the marked lines to quilt the fabric. Cut a 20cm/8in square from the finished piece and fold in half, right sides together. Pin along the bottom and side edges, then machine stitch 1cm/½in from the edge. Neaten with zigzag stitch then turn right side out.

6 Cut a 20cm/8in length of ribbon, press in half and stitch over the raw edges. Hand sew a rocaille bead at every point where two quilting lines cross. Hand sew ribbon roses below the opening.

Use a small piece of marbled silk to cover a ready-made headband. The silk is cut on the cross grain so that it will stretch round the curved shape of the headband.

Marbled Headband

1 Prepare a shallow dye bath and add the marbling thickening medium, following the manufacturer's instructions. Using a fine artist's paintbrush, scatter drops of dye on to the surface. When the surface is covered with colour, drag a cocktail stick or toothpick through the dye at regular intervals, vertically then horizontally, to break up the dye and create a pattern.

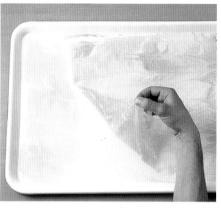

2 Gently place the silk on to the marbled surface, placing the top or the centre on first. When the silk has soaked up the dye, peel it away and rinse under cool water to remove the thickening medium. Leave to dry, then iron to fix (set) the dye, following the manufacturer's instructions.

3 Cut a strip of the marbled silk diagonally across the grain, at least twice the width of the headband.

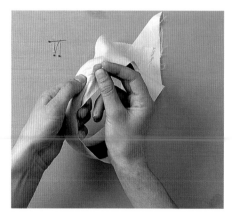

4 Remove the lining from the inside curve of the headband. Pin the strip of silk to one end. Stretching the fabric gently around the outside of the curve, pin the other end of the silk to the other end of the headband.

5 Trim the edges to 2cm/¾in wider than the headband on each side. Coat the inside curve of the headband with adhesive, then glue the raw edges down, mitring the corners. Glue the original lining back in position.

Soak pieces of blanket in tea bags and brown dye, then use them to make a soft, appealing cover for a child's hot water bottle. A draw-string cord holds the cover in place.

Tea-dyed Hot Water Bottle Cover

you will need

2–3 tea bags

dye baths

rubber gloves

old blanket or wool fabric, pre-washed

iron

cloth

brown hand dye

hot water bottle

pencil and paper

scissors

tailor's chalk

sewing machine

matching sewing thread

1.5cm/⅝in-wide brown ribbon

satin bias binding (optional)

1m/1yd fine brown cord

safety pin

vanishing fabric marker

stranded embroidery thread (floss)

embroidery needle

tiny buttons

needle

1 Soak two or three tea bags in hot water in a small dye bath until the tea is quite strong. Immerse a small piece of the old blanket or wool fabric. Agitate until you are happy with the colour, re-dyeing if necessary. Allow to dry and press under a damp cloth.

2 Dye a larger piece of fabric for the hot water bottle cover using brown hand dye and following the manufacturer's instructions. Dry and press under a damp cloth.

3 Using a hot water bottle, make a paper template for the cover. Fold the brown fabric in half. Place the template on top, then draw around it with tailor's chalk. Cut out a rectangular back and front large enough to fit the hot water bottle.

4 On the wrong side of each front and back, stitch a length of ribbon about 5cm/2in below the top short raw edge. Using a 1cm/½in seam allowance, stitch the back and front together, leaving a gap just below the ribbon. Bind the long raw edges. Fold in the bag top so that the ribbon is at the top edge of the bag, and stitch.

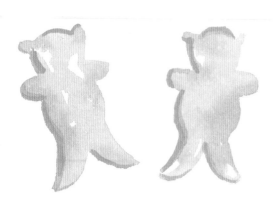

 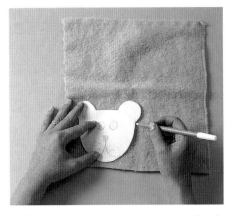 

5 Cut the cord in half. Using a safety pin, thread one piece through a side opening, around the casing and out through the same opening. Knot the ends. Repeat with the second piece of cord through the second side opening.

6 Enlarge the teddy motif at the back of the book to fit the tea-dyed fabric. Draw around the template using a vanishing fabric marker. Cut out a face. Draw in the features on the teddy's face.

7 Hand embroider the features using stranded embroidery thread (floss). Add small buttons for the eyes. Slip stitch the face to the bag front, taking care not to catch the back of the cover in the stitching.

Dip-dyeing lengthways and then widthways creates subtle blends of colour, but choose your colours carefully to avoid a "muddy" effect. Finish these simple mats with contrast ribbon borders.

Double-dyed Place Mats

you will need

scissors

white cotton fabric

cold water hand dyes, in 3 colours

large dye bath

rubber gloves

clothes pegs (pins)

iron

ribbon, in contrast colours

dressmaker's pins

needle

tacking (basting) thread

embroidery thread (floss)

needle

1 Cut the fabric to the desired size for each mat, cutting along the grain of the fabric to ensure a square edge. The fabric may fray during dyeing, so allow 1–2cm/½–¾in wastage. Prepare the first dye bath following the manufacturer's instructions. Dampen the fabric with water.

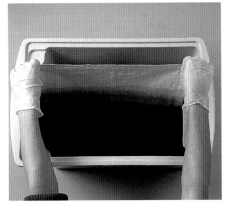

2 Holding the fabric lengthways, dip each rectangle no more than two-thirds into the bath. When the fabric is the desired colour (it will become more intense the longer it is in the dye), remove it and rinse in cold water until the water runs clear.

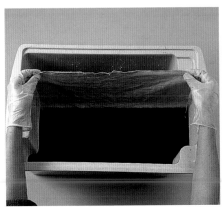

3 Prepare the second dye bath. While the fabric is still damp, dip each rectangle in the dye bath lengthways so that the undyed area is submerged. Prepare the third dye bath.

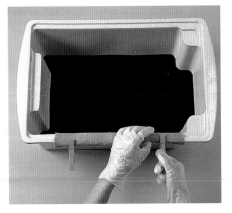

4 Dip each mat widthways so that half of it is submerged. Peg (pin) the fabric to the edge of the dye bath. This colour will cover both of the previously dyed colours, creating subtle colour blends. Wash the mats using a mild detergent, and rinse until the water runs clear. Iron while damp.

5 Trim the edges of each mat. Press the ribbon in half lengthways and pin around the outside of the mat so that the crease lies on the edge. Tack (baste) in place. Using embroidery thread (floss), work blanket stitch through the edge of the ribbon to hold it in place. Remove the tacking.

To create this tie-dye design on plain handkerchiefs, simply fold them then dip the edges of the pleated folds briefly in two dye colours. The result is a striking chequerboard pattern.

Folded Silk Handkerchiefs

you will need
white or pale-coloured silk
handkerchiefs, pre-washed
iron
dye bath
powder dyes, in 2 colours
absorbent cloth or paper
brown craft or lining paper

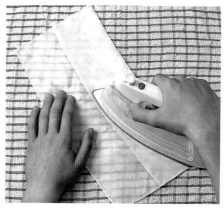

1 Wash each piece of fabric in mild detergent to remove any dressing. Pleat the handkerchief accordion-style into quarters and press the folds.

2 Prepare a dye bath with the first colour dye, following the manufacturer's instructions. You will only need a small amount of dye. Turn each pleated handkerchief so that a row of folds points down, then dip the edge very briefly in the dye.

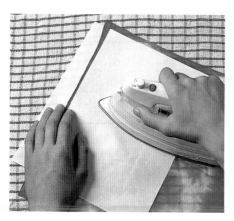

3 Place each handkerchief on an absorbent piece of cloth or paper, then carefully open out flat to dry. Place each handkerchief flat between two pieces of brown craft or lining paper, and press with a warm, dry iron. Remove from the paper.

4 Pleat the handkerchiefs with the folds at right angles to the previous ones, across the lines of dye. Press each fold. Prepare the dye bath with the second colour, then dip the handkerchiefs as before. Leave to dry and press as in step 3.

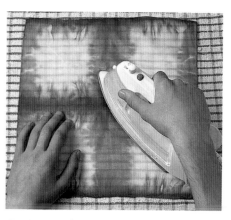

5 Rinse the handkerchiefs in cold water until the water runs clear. Then wash in lukewarm water using a mild detergent. Iron the handkerchiefs flat while still damp.

Neatly pressed pleats create this simple design, which is then bound with fine cord or string to create the tie-dye effect. Only one shade of dye is used on coloured fabric.

Pleated Table Runner

you will need
iron
lilac silk dupion, pre-washed
ruler
scissors
fine cord or string
rubber gloves
dye bath
blue hand dye
needle
matching sewing thread

1 Iron the washed silk while still damp. Cut to the size required for your table (the length should include the fringe), allowing 4.5cm/1¾in wastage on all sides.

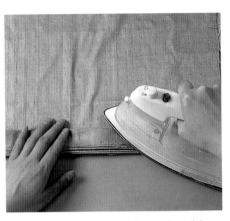

2 Using an iron, pleat the fabric accordion fashion, making each pleat about 3cm/1¼in wide. If your runner is very long, horizontal pleats may become unmanageable, so you may prefer to make the pleats vertically.

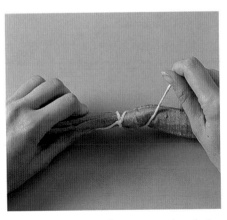

3 Using fine cord or string, bind the fabric tightly along the pleats, spacing each binding about 7.5cm/3in apart. Start in the centre and work out towards the edges.

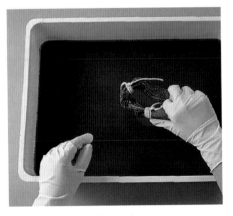

4 Wearing rubber gloves, prepare a dye bath big enough to allow the fabric to move freely. Dampen the tied cloth before placing it in the bath. Dye the fabric according to the manufacturer's instructions. When it is the desired colour, remove it and rinse under cold water until the water runs clear. Remove the bindings and wash to remove any dye.

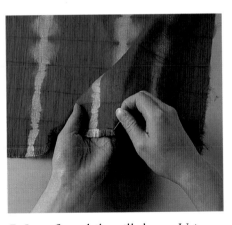

5 Iron flat while still damp. Using a needle, make a fringe at each short end by pulling out the weft threads to about 4cm/1½in deep. Fold the cloth in half to ensure that it is square, then trim 2.5cm/1in from each long side. Press under a 1cm/½in double hem on each long side, then slip stitch it neatly in place. Trim the ends of the fringe level at each end.

Cover a selection of notebooks, a shoebox and a cardboard tube with marbled fabric to make a co-ordinating desk set. The metal fittings add a traditional look.

Marbled Fabric Desk Set

you will need
large shallow dye bath
marbling thickening medium
rubber gloves
marbling dyes, in black and white
small pointed instrument such as
a skewer
scissors
cotton sateen fabric
double-sided tape
2 short lengths of square
wooden dowel
notebooks, shoebox and large
cardboard tube
strong fabric glue
metal label frames
bradawl
pop rivet tool and metal rivets

1 Fill the dye bath with cold water to a depth of about 5cm/2in. Add the marbling thickening medium. Wearing rubber gloves, drop a small amount of black marbling paint on to the surface.

2 Drop a small amount of white marbling paint on to the surface of the black paint.

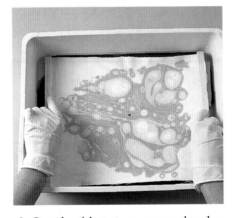

4 Cut the fabric into rectangles that will fit into the dye bath. Using double-sided tape, attach each end of the first piece of fabric to a length of wooden dowel; this will hold the fabric flat and make it easier to handle. Holding the dowels, gently arrange the fabric, right side down, on to the surface of the water.

5 Lift the fabric carefully, then untape the dowels and hang up to dry. Repeat with the remaining fabric until you have enough to cover the desk set.

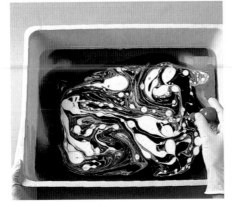

3 Using a small pointed instrument, gently mix the two colours into a swirly marbled pattern.

6 To cover the large notebook, apply strips of double-sided tape to the book cover. Take a piece of fabric about 5cm/2in larger all round than the notebook and wrap it around it, pressing firmly. Snip across each corner. Apply fabric glue to the exposed edges, then stick them to the inside. Place a metal label frame on the front. Pierce a hole through each fixing (attachment) point, using a bradawl. Use a pop rivet tool and rivets to hold the metal frame in place.

7 For the pen pot, cut a piece of fabric 5cm/2in deeper than the cardboard tube and 1cm/½in longer than its circumference. Fold and glue a small hem along the lower edge. Apply fabric glue to the tube, then wrap the fabric round it. Glue down the overlap. Snip tabs into the excess fabric at the top. Apply glue to the inside of the tube, then fold the tabs into the inside.

Fold a small piece of silk neatly in accordion fashion and secure with rubber bands before dyeing it in a single colour. The dyed silk is then machine quilted to protect your jewellery.

Tie-dyed Jewellery Roll

you will need

dye bath

powder dye

40 x 100cm/16 x 40in wild silk

rubber bands

iron

scissors

large piece of wadding (batting)

needle

tacking (basting) thread

sewing machine

matching sewing thread

satin bias binding, in contrast colour

dressmaker's pins

15cm/6in zipper

poppers (snap fasteners)

1 Prepare a hot or cold-water dye bath of the desired colour, following the dye manufacturer's instructions.

2 Pleat the silk accordion fashion and bind it twice, using rubber bands. Dampen the bundle then place it in the dye bath. Keep the fabric moving in the dye to get an even colour.

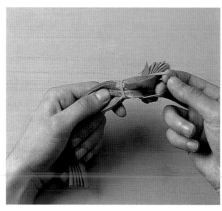

3 When the desired colour has been achieved, remove the fabric and rinse under cold water. While the silk is still damp, remove the rubber bands and wash the fabric in warm water using a mild detergent. Iron the silk flat while it is still damp.

4 Cut two pieces 18 x 40cm/7 x 16in from the dyed silk. Cut a piece of wadding (batting) the same size and sandwich it between the two pieces of silk. Tack (baste) the layers together. Machine quilt the layers together to create a meandering quilted effect. Cut three strips of bias binding 17cm/6½in long. Position one strip along each short end of the quilted silk, fold over and pin.

5 Stitch the zipper to the underside of one short bound edge. Fold in each short end of the quilted silk by 7.5cm/3in and pin in place. Divide the end of the roll without the zipper into three equally sized pockets by stitching two lines the depth of the turn-over.

6 Position the remaining bias binding strip over the raw edge of the zipper and stitch the long sides in place.

7 For the tie, cut two strips of binding, one 20cm/8in and the other 6cm/2½in. Fold in half widthways and top stitch all around.

8 Stitch half of a popper (snap fastener) to one end of each tie. Stitch a short end of each tie to the side edges of the roll. Cut strips of bias binding to fit the long edges and pin in place Tuck in the raw edges at each end. Stitch in place, then slipstitch the short ends.

Decorate the rim of a dip-dyed silk lampshade with delicate embroidery thread (floss) tassels, dip-dyeing the tip of each tassel to complement the colour used on the shade.

Tassel-edged Lampshade

you will need

dye bath

dark green cold-water dye

small silk lampshade

absorbent cloth or paper

scissors

thin cardboard

embroidery thread (floss), to match the lampshade

silk thread, to match the dye colour

small bowl

small beads

pencil or tailor's chalk

tape measure

dressmaker's glue

1 Prepare a dye bath, following the dye manufacturer's instructions. Dip the bottom edge of the lampshade briefly in the dye bath so that one-quarter is submerged. Stand it on an absorbent cloth or paper for a few minutes to remove any excess dye. Turn it upside down and leave to dry. Repeat if you would prefer to build up a darker colour.

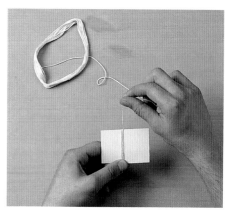

2 To make the tassels, cut a piece of thin cardboard slightly wider than the desired length of the tassels and wind the embroidery thread (floss) around it. These tassels were made by winding the thread ten times, but you can vary the number of wraps to make thicker or thinner tassels.

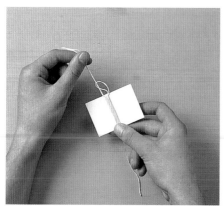

3 Cut another piece of thread about 20cm/8in long. Pass this through the loop of threads as shown. Knot the thread tightly around the loop to hold the threads tightly.

4 Using sharp scissors, cut the wrapped threads and trim evenly.

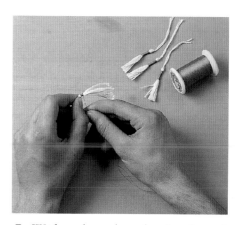

5 With a long length of coloured silk thread, bind the top of the folded-over lengths of tassel. Knot and leave the ends hanging the length of the tassel. Make enough tassels to go round the shade.

6 Prepare a dye bath slightly darker than the one used for the lampshade. Dip the tip of each tassel in the dye and leave to dry on absorbent cloth.

7 String a bead on to the looped thread at the top of each tassel, and tie a small knot to hold it in place. Cut the remaining thread down to 1cm/½in. Trim the tassels evenly.

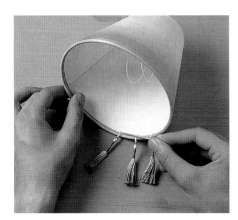

8 Using a pencil or tailor's chalk, make evenly spaced marks on the inside edge of the lampshade. Using dressmaker's glue, attach a tassel to each mark inside the rim.

Using fabric etching medium, draw a design that destroys the silk pile of velvet but leaves the backing fabric intact. The dyed velvet makes a lovely blind, with the light filtering through the etched pattern.

Velvet Blind

you will need

tracing paper and pencil

black felt-tipped pen

white silk/viscose velvet

masking tape

vanishing fabric marker

set square (t-square)

silk pins (push pins)

painting frame

fabric etching medium

hairdryer

iron

tape measure

scissors

lilac hand dye

large dye bath

rubber gloves

satin bias binding

sewing machine

matching sewing thread

roller blind kit

1 Enlarge the template to the required size. Outline it with a black pen. Tape the velvet, pile side down, to the work surface. Using a vanishing fabric marker and a set square (t-square), mark up the blind with a grid to fit the template.

2 Place the design underneath the velvet and trace it with the vanishing fabric marker. Move the template and repeat until the whole grid has been filled in.

3 Using silk pins, stretch the fabric on a painting frame, with the pile upwards. Trace over the design with fabric etching medium, following the manufacturer's instructions. Keep your movements fast to prevent the lines becoming too thick. (Practise on a spare piece of fabric first.)

4 Dry the etching medium with a hairdryer to burn away the pile. Once it is dry, iron the fabric on the wrong side using a cool iron. Trim any wastage from around the edge so that the velvet is the exact size required for the blind.

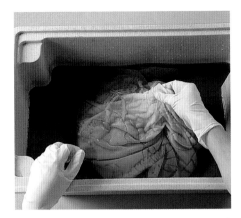

5 Place the fabric in water to reveal the design, rubbing the surface if necessary to remove any unwanted fibres. Dye the blind to the required shade while the fabric is still damp, using hand dye and following the manufacturer's instructions. Hang out to dry.

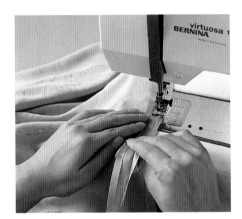

6 Open up a piece of bias binding long enough to run down the side of the blind. Machine stitch it to the wrong side. Fold the binding over to the right side of the blind and top stitch close to the edge of the binding. Trim the top and bottom of the bound edge level with the top and bottom of the blind. Repeat on the other side.

7 Bind the bottom, leaving 1cm/½in extra at each end of the binding. Fold this in, then top stitch to give neat corners. Complete the blind, using a roller blind kit.

Children will love this strong fake fur and cotton cushion, measuring 70cm/28in across x 20cm/8in high. Two contrast dye colours have been used to dip-dye the fabric.

Doughnut Floor Cushion

you will need

80cm/32in-square of paper
ruler or tape measure
50cm/20in length of string
soft pencil
scissors
dressmaker's pins
1m/1yd white acrylic fake fur fabric
1m/1yd heavy white cotton fabric
rubber gloves
cold water dyes, in turquoise and red
dye bath
sewing machine
matching sewing threads
bag polystyrene (styrofoam) pellets
large cup or beaker

1 Fold the paper into quarters. Loop the string around a pencil 7.5cm/3in from one end. Hold the end of the string in the corner of the paper and draw an arc from fold to fold. Lengthen the loop to 35cm/14in and draw another arc. Open out the pattern and pin it to the fake fur. Cut one shape. Cut another from cotton.

2 Measure the two circumferences and add 10cm/4in to each measurement. Cut three lengths of cotton, each 20cm/8in wide, two for the outside edge and one for the inside edge of the doughnut. On the wrong side of each piece of fabric, mark the halfway line with a soft pencil.

3 Wearing rubber gloves, mix each dye in a bath, following the manufacturer's instructions. Dampen each fabric piece to within 2cm/¾in of the halfway line. Dip one edge of damp fabric into the turquoise dye bath, leaving the other half outside. Remove the fabric, allowing the dye to drip back into the bath. Allow to drip dry.

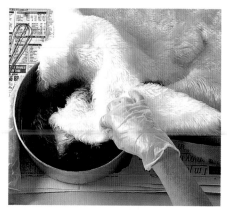

4 Dip the undyed half of each piece of fabric into the red dye in the same way. Leave a 2–3cm/¾–1¼in gap between the two colours so that they do not bleed into each other.

5 With right sides together, fold one inside edge side panel in half and stitch the 20cm/8in ends together for the inner circle. Pin one edge of the inside circle to the inside edge of the fur circle. Stitch in place. Zigzag stitch the raw edges. Pin and stitch the two outer sides together into a loop. Pin and stitch the outer side to the fur circle. Turn inside out, pin and stitch the outer edge of the base to the cotton circle. Finish the edges with zigzag stitch. Carefully turn the cushion right side out.

6 Turn in the inside raw edges. Whip stitch the inside circle to the hole in the bottom of the cushion, leaving a 15cm/6in opening. Pour in the polystyrene (styrofoam) pellets to fill the cushion. Stitch the opening shut.

Machine stitch large blue-and-white tie-dyed squares on to a plain white duvet cover for a bold modern look. Vary the stripes and circles to add extra interest to the design.

Tie-dyed Duvet Cover

you will need

iron

white cotton and linen fabrics with contrasting textures, pre-washed

coins, marbles and beads

rubber bands

strong thread or string

blue machine or hand dye

dye bath (optional)

set square (t-square)

scissors

needle

tacking (basting) thread

white duvet cover

vanishing fabric marker

dressmaker's pins

sewing machine

matching sewing thread

1 Iron the cotton and linen fabrics flat while still damp. Tie circular items of different sizes, such as coins, marbles or beads, into half of the fabric pieces, securing them tightly with rubber bands.

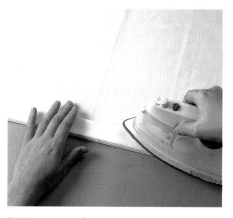

2 To create the stripe effect, pleat the remaining fabric accordion fashion, with the pleats about 3cm/1¼in wide. Bind the pleated roll of fabric, using strong thread or string. Space the ties evenly on each piece of fabric, but vary the spacing between pieces of cloth to give interesting stripes of different proportions.

3 Dye the tied bundles, following the manufacturer's instructions. Remove the bindings and rinse away all excess dye. Iron the fabrics flat while they are still damp.

4 Cut the dyed fabrics into 27cm/ 11in squares, which includes a 1cm/½in seam allowance on all sides. Turn under the seam allowance and tack (baste), mitring the corners neatly. Press each square.

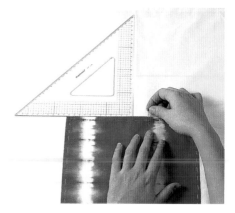

5 Iron a crease down the centre of the duvet cover. Measure and mark with a vanishing marker 25cm/10in down the central crease from the top seam. Centre the first square on the crease, with the top edge on the 25cm/10in mark. Pin in position.

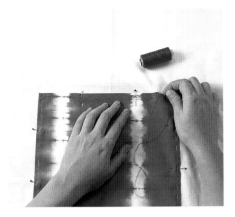 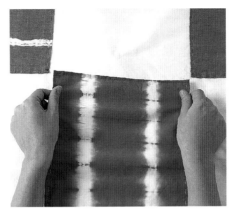 

6 Position the rest of the top row, placing them one square's width from each other horizontally. Tack (baste) in place.

7 Pin, then tack the remaining tie-dyed squares, making sure they are all square to each other and to the sides of the duvet cover.

8 Machine stitch round each square close to the edge. Remove the tacking threads. Wash the cover according to the dye manufacturer's instructions.

Tie-dyeing works well on rich fabrics such as velvet and silk-satin. Bind patches of different fabrics round circular objects such as buttons and beads, then assemble the patchwork by hand.

Tie-dyed Patchwork Cushion

you will need

small piece of cardboard

ruler

scissors

selection of light-coloured fabrics (e.g. velvet, silk dupion, silk-satin)

vanishing marker pen

coins, lentils, buttons and beads

rubber bands

rubber gloves

cold water hand dyes, in 4 colours

dye bath

iron

stiff paper

dressmaker's pins

needle

tacking (basting) thread

matching sewing thread

cushion pad

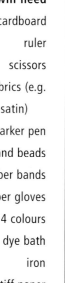

1 Divide the dimensions of the cushion front and back by the required number of patches. Add on 2cm/¾in all round and cut out a cardboard template to that size. Cut the required number of squares using the template as a guide. In the centre of each, place a circular object such as a button or coin and bind securely with a rubber band. Divide the bundles into four, putting a mix of fabrics in each pile.

2 Wearing rubber gloves, prepare each dye bath following the dye manufacturer's instructions, then immerse the bundles for the specified length of time. Rinse in cold water until the water runs clear. Remove the bindings and wash the squares in warm water using mild detergent.

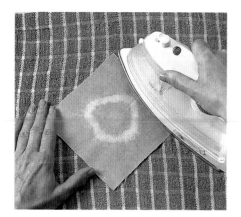

3 Iron the fabric flat while still damp. Trim the fabric squares by 1cm/½in all around.

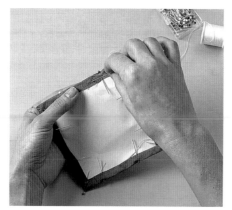

4 Cut away 2cm/¾in all around the cardboard template. Use it to make paper templates. Centre a template on the wrong side of each square. Fold in the excess fabric and pin.

5 Mitre the corners and tack (baste) around the edge, stitching through the fabric and the paper. Arrange the squares into a rectangle four squares wide by eight squares long, which, when folded in half, will make up the front and back of the cushion cover. Ensure that you are happy with the arrangement of colours.

6 Oversew all the squares right sides together. Sew the mitred corners in place, except on those that appear around the outside edge of the rectangle. Remove the tacking threads and the templates, then press the seams flat under a damp cloth. Fold the patchwork in half, right sides together, and stitch along two sides.

7 Fold over the seam allowance on the open side and tack. Turn the cover through to the right side and insert the cushion pad. Pin, then sew the open side closed.

Make a set of fine cotton napkins using just one colour of dye and hand folding the fabric into small pleated parcels. Make a tablecloth or tablemats to match if you like.

Folded Napkin Parcels

you will need

scissors

ruler or set square (t-square)

fine white cotton fabric

dressmaker's pins

needle

tacking (basting) thread

sewing machine

white sewing thread

large bodkin or safety pin

iron

thick string

hand dye

glass bowl (for microwave method)

clear film (plastic wrap) (for microwave method)

dye bath (for hand method)

rubber gloves

1 Cut six squares each 35cm/14in and six strips 35 x 5cm/14 x 2in from the cotton fabric. Pin and tack (baste) under a narrow double hem on all four sides of each square. Fold each strip in half lengthways and tack, then machine stitch about 1cm/½in from the raw edge, leaving a small gap in the stitching halfway along the length. Use a large bodkin or safety pin to turn each strip to the right side. Press flat. Stitch the gap.

2 Find the centre of each strip and pin it to one edge of each square, about halfway along. Stitch the hem in place close to the innermost folded edge, stitching over the strip. Press the hem.

5 Prepare a dye bath following the manufacturer's instructions and microwave for 4 minutes. Alternatively leave the parcels submerged for 45 minutes. Wearing rubber gloves, remove the parcels and rinse. Remove the string and rinse again until the water runs clear. Iron while still damp.

3 Fold each napkin into pleats about 4cm/1½in wide, then press flat using your hands.

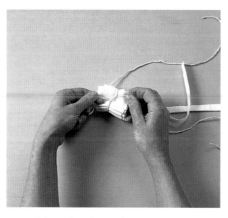

4 Fold each pleated napkin again to form a small square parcel. Tie up the napkin parcel tightly using a length of thick string.

Tie-dyed silk fabrics make a luxurious lightweight bedcover. Vary the objects tied into the patches and the binding materials, as well as the size of the patches.

Tie-dyed Patchwork Bedspread

you will need
ruler
pencil
white paper
scissors
vanishing marker pen
selection of silk fabrics, pre-washed
beads, buttons, coins, lentils, etc.
binding materials (e.g. cord, string)
dye bath
powder dyes, in 4 or more colours
absorbent cloth or paper
iron
protective cloth or lining paper
dressmaker's pins
fine needle
tacking (basting) thread
matching sewing thread
1.5 x 1.8m/5 x 6ft cotton backing
fabric or sheet
sewing machine

1 To make a bedspread 1.5 x 1.8m (5 x 6ft), you will need three patch sizes: 15 squares each 30cm/12in, 30 squares each 15cm/6in, and 30 rectangles 30 x 15cm/12 x 6in. Make a paper template as a guide, then cut the required number from fabric adding a 1cm/½in seam allowance all round.

2 Tie different circular objects into the fabric patches. Bind them with various cords and strings to vary the tie-dyed results.

3 Prepare each dye bath, following the manufacturer's instructions, and dye one-quarter of the material in each bath. Wash each patch in warm water, using a mild detergent. Remove the objects and rinse until the water runs clear. Leave to dry on absorbent cloth or paper.

4 Steam iron each patch. Turn in each seam allowance using a paper template as a guide. Pin and tack (baste) the seam firmly in place.

5 Using a neat overstitch, hand stitch two small patches together to make a rectangle. Continue joining the small squares together until you have 15 bicoloured rectangles.

6 Sew a pieced rectangle to a single rectangle, to form a 30cm/12in square. Continue joining rectangles until you have a total of 15 squares. Sew a patchwork square to a solid square.

7 Continue joining squares in this way to make a row of five squares, alternating patchwork squares with solid ones. Arrange in six rows, start-ing three rows with a patched square and three with a solid one. Sew the rows together. Remove the tacking threads and the paper templates. Press the seams flat. Pin the backing fabric to the patchwork, right sides together. Machine stitch round three sides. Turn the bedspread through, then pin and stitch the open side closed.

In this complex marbling design, extra colours are added on top of each other and then carefully dragged out to create petal-like shapes. The background marbling is done using a handmade comb.

Marbled Book Cover

you will need

masking tape
dressmaker's pins
wooden batten or ruler
shallow dye bath
marbling thickening medium
marbling dyes
pipette (eye-dropper)
fine artist's paintbrush
wooden cocktail stick (toothpick)
scissors
crêpe de chine silk, pre-washed
tape measure
book, photo album or diary
absorbent cloth or paper
iron
tape
sewing machine
matching sewing thread
needle

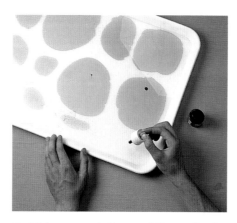

1 Make a comb for marbling a feathery pattern by taping dressmaker's pins along the edge of a wooden batten or a ruler. Prepare a shallow dye bath with marbling thickening medium (see Techniques). Using a pipette (eye-dropper), place eight drops of each background dye colour on to the surface, allowing room for each colour to spread.

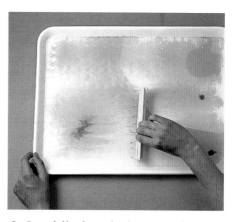

2 Carefully drag the homemade comb several times across the surface, backwards and forwards, horizontally and vertically, to create a feathery pattern.

3 Add to the design by applying drops of a contrasting colour dye to the surface of the dye bath, allowing them to spread outwards.

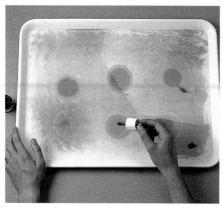

4 Apply different-coloured drops to the centre of each circle.

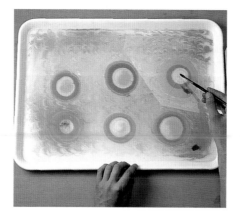

5 Continue applying colour to the centre of each circle, until you have as many colours as you want.

6 Around each circle, drag the point of a toothpick from the outside edge towards the centre, to form petal-like shapes. Drag the point of the stick from within the petals past the outside edges to create points.

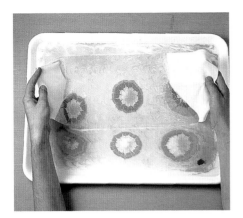

7 Cut two pieces of fabric 1.5cm/⅝in larger than the opened book size. Place each in turn on the surface of the inked solution.

8 When the silk has soaked up the dye, peel it away and rinse under cool water to remove the thickening medium. Place on absorbent cloth or paper to dry, then press with a warm, dry iron to fix (set) the dye, following the manufacturer's instructions.

9 Place one piece of silk right side down. Centre the opened book, cover side down on top. Fold the fabric edges in and tape them to the inside of the cover, mitring the corners.

10 For the book flaps, from the remaining dyed silk, cut two pieces, each the size of the inside cover plus 2cm/1in seam allowances all around. Press under a 1cm/½in seam all round, then stitch the fold along one short edge. With right sides together and raw edges aligned, pin each flap to the outside edges of the outer cover. Ensure the machine-stitched edge faces the centre of the book. Hand stitch the other three sides in place.

Space-dyeing

Natural fabrics and yarns can be dyed with several colours at once, giving wonderful random rainbow colours and magical effects. Once you have experimented with ready-made dyes, you can progress to making up your own dye recipes. Dyes can be painted on to the fabric with a brush, sprayed on with a water mister or sprinkled using a pepperpot. Alternatively, dampened fabric can be coloured in a dye bath with several colours together.

Random Reactions

In most dyeing techniques the aim is to submerge the fabric completely with plenty of room in the dye bath so that the fibres take up the colour evenly. Space-dyeing employs a different technique. By deliberately crumpling the fabric instead of spreading it out, and using several different colour dyes at once in the same dye bath, a random multi-coloured pattern will emerge. The more the fabric is crumpled, the greater the patterning will be. Until the dyeing is completed and the fabric is dry, the outcome cannot be predicted so this technique is stimulating to experiment with.

To make sure all the fabric is dyed you need to cover all the white parts with the various dye solutions, but do not stir them together in case the colours merge and become "muddy". Different kinds of

dye are suitable for different fabrics – acid dyes (where the acid is a white vinegar), for instance, are used for wool and silk, but not for cotton or linen. Fabrics such as silk react very quickly to the dye, while others take much longer. Space-dyeing

produces vibrant colours on fabrics such as cotton and silk, but used on a delicate fabric such as muslin (cheesecloth) it will give a pastel look. Follow the instructions in the Techniques section for achieving pale or deep colours, as specified in each project.

As well as space-dyeing fabrics, embroidery threads (floss) and woollen yarns can also be dyed. These random-dyed threads look wonderful mixed together in a piece of embroidery. Reactive dyes can be painted directly on to the fabric, then sealed  in a plastic bag to fix (set). Alternatively, spray on the dyes, using cut-out

paper shapes or bands of tape to mask off areas of plain fabric to make a design.

If you are using a dye bath, this will dictate the size of the fabric you can dye, so if you have only a small dye bath, create larger finished projects by using the patchwork technique to join fabric pieces together. Another idea is to decorate a large area of plain fabric such as a tablecloth or pelmet with small pieces of spray-dyed fabric.

The appeal of space-dyeing is its random colouring effect. The dye bath for this technique need not be large, as fabric is crumpled to allow the different dyes to blend together in the fabric.

Materials

Polyester toy stuffing

Light and resilient, this can be used for stuffing small shapes.

Salt

Common salt is needed for some reactive dyeing methods.

Threads (floss) and yarns

Try dyeing silk and wool thread for embroidery, or cotton lace, viscose cord and cotton or viscose fringing for sewing projects.

Urea

This is used in solution to help dissolve the dye in strong solutions. It also allows greater dye penetration when spray-dyeing and fabric painting with reactive dyes.

Washing soda (sodium carbonate)

Use washing soda to fix reactive dyes. Dissolve 100g/3½oz washing soda crystals in 500ml/18fl oz boiling water. Stir well and allow to cool.

Washing-up (dishwashing) liquid

Use to soak fabric and threads before dyeing, and for setting cotton. A neutral pH detergent is useful, as it prevents any unfixed dye being picked up by another part of the fabric.

White vinegar

This is used to fix acid dyes.

Beads

Use these for decoration.

Bonding powder (fusible web)

This is used to bond two fabrics together with heat.

Dyes

Acid dyes (using white vinegar) are used for wool and silk, cold-water reactive dyes for cotton, viscose and silk. Special fabric paints and printing inks are also available.

Fabrics

These include natural fabrics such as cotton poplin, wool and silk, and manmade fabrics. All cotton, except velvet, should be machine washed at 60°C/140°F, then dried. Wool and silk should be dampened in warm water with washing-up liquid added before dyeing.

Non-woven interfacing

Available in a range of weights, including pelmet weight.

While fabric that is dyed using space-dyeing methods appears spontaneous, the dyes and chemical solutions are carefully weighed out. Accurate measuring equipment is very important in space-dyeing.

Equipment

Baking paper (parchment paper)
Protect the ironing board with a cloth while ironing fabric dry. Use baking paper to protect the iron.

Clothes pegs (pins)
Use to seal dyed fabric in plastic bags.

Dye bath
Dye baths for cold-water reactive dye methods can be plastic. Use a heat-proof container for hot-water dyes. Use a metal dye bath for acid dyes.

Glass jars with lids
Use to make and store dye solutions.

Iron
Press damp dyed fabrics dry. Use to press fabrics.

Measuring beaker
Use to measure dye solutions and add water to make up volume.

Measuring spoon
Use to measure dye powders.

Pepperpot (pepper shaker)
Use to sprinkle reactive dyes on to dampened fabric.

Plastic bags
Use to seal a dye bath, using clothes pegs (pins).

Plastic piping
Use to roll up dye-painted fabric before sealing in a plastic bag.

Plastic sheet
Use a large plastic sheet to protect your work surface, especially when painting with dyes.

Rubber gloves
Wear to avoid staining your hands.

Scales and measuring spoons
Use scales to weigh dry fabric. Use measuring spoons for dyes and beakers and syringes for measuring liquids.

Stirring rods
Use glass or plastic rods, or lengths of bamboo, to mix dye solutions.

Syringe
Use to measure very accurate quantities of dye solution.

Thermometer
Use to check temperature of hot water dye bath while heating.

When space-dyeing with cold water dyes, it is best to use no more than 3–4 times the volume of liquid to the weight of the fabric. To dye 100g/3½oz fabric, use up to 400ml/14fl oz total liquid.

Techniques

Preparing soda solution and cold-water reactive dyes

Cold water reactive dyes remain usable for about a week after they have been made up. After that they lose strength. Store in a sealed jar.

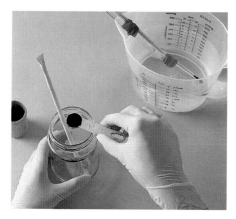

1 To make a soda solution, dissolve 100g/3½oz washing soda crystals (sodium carbonate) in 500ml/18fl oz boiling water. Stir well then leave to cool.

2 To make a stock dye solution, pour 300ml/½ pint cold water into a glass jar, mark the level around the jar and pour the water away.

3 Measure 2.5ml/½ tsp dye powder into the jar. Add a few drops of cold water and stir to a paste. Pour hot water (not more than 60°C/140°F) into the jar up to the mark and stir thoroughly until the dye is dissolved.

Pepperpot (pepper shaker) method with reactive dyes

The pepperpot method of dyeing fabric produces a subtle speckled effect of comets and tails on the fabric surface.

1 Dissolve 25g/1oz salt in 100ml/3½fl oz hot water. Leave to cool, then measure 25ml/1½ tbsp salt solution and 40ml/1½fl oz soda solution into a jar. Make the mixture up to 150ml/¼ pint with cold water.

2 Cut a piece of dry fabric from your project instructions to fit into the bottom of a deep plastic tray. Paint with the salt and soda solution until damp but not too wet.

3 Put small amounts of up to three powdered cold-water reactive dyes into pepperpots (pepper shakers).

4 Shake the dye sparingly on to the fabric, a small amount at a time. Leave for a minute between applications, as the colour will develop quite quickly. Leave for 30 minutes to 1 hour. Remove the fabric from the dye bath and rinse until the water runs clear. Wash in hot soapy water, then rinse again. Iron the fabric dry.

Cold-water reactive space-dyeing method for pale colours

When fabric has been coloured with reactive dyes, rinse it thoroughly until the water runs clear. Wash in water with washing-up (dishwashing) liquid, leave to dry partially, then iron dry.

1 Weigh the fabric to be dyed, then soak in warm water with a little washing-up (dishwashing) liquid added for at least 30 minutes. Squeeze out the excess water and crumple the fabric in the dye bath.

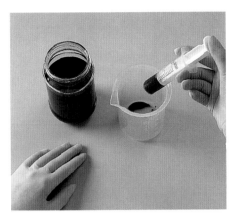

2 For each colour used, measure the amount of dye solution needed with a syringe and pour into a measuring beaker. Refer to the recipe, and add the amount of water required.

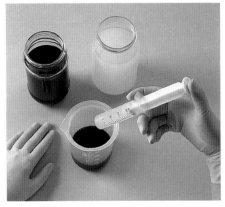

3 Measure the soda solution (sodium carbonate) needed and pour into the beaker containing dye solution. Once this has been added, the dye solution must be used fairly quickly, as it will lose its strength within a couple of hours of making.

4 Pour the solutions carefully over the fabric in the dye bath. (Dye baths for cold water reactive dye methods can be plastic.) Try to cover all white parts, but do not stir or the colours may become muddy.

5 Leave for at least one hour at room temperature, then rinse thoroughly until the water runs clear. Wash in hot water with a little washing-up liquid added, then rinse again. Allow the fabric to dry partially and then iron completely dry. It is ready for use after airing.

Spray-dyeing

Measure 2.5ml/½ tsp dye into a glass. Stir to a paste with cold water. Make up to 300ml/½ pint with chemical water and stir well. Measure 20ml/ 4 tsp of this solution into a spray bottle. Add an equal amount of soda solution. Spray the fabric, allowing a few minutes' rest between colours to let the colour spread. Spray evenly over the whole piece, or concentrate colours in particular areas. Areas may be masked by pinning paper shapes to the fabric after one colour has been sprayed and then spraying another colour. Remove the masks and allow the fabric to dry overnight. Press with a hot iron. Wash the fabric in hot soapy water, allow to dry then iron again.

Cold water reactive space-dyeing method for deep colours

If very strong solutions or dyes are needed, you may prefer to make them up in chemical water. This helps the dye to dissolve but does not affect the colour or depth of shade.

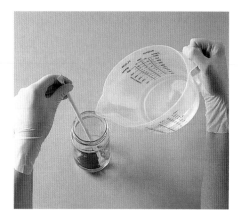

1 If very strong solutions of dye are needed, you may prefer to make them up in chemical water. This helps the dye dissolve but does not affect the colour or depth of shade. To make chemical water, weigh out 120g/4oz urea and make up to 1 litre/1¾ pints with hot water. Stir well and allow to cool. Make the dye into a paste with cold water, then make up to 300ml/ ½ pint with chemical water.

2 Spread out the fabric in a plastic dye bath. The more crumpled the fabric is, the greater the patterning will be.

3 Measure the chemical dye solution according to the recipe and add the soda solution (sodium carbonate) as before. Pour the solutions carefully over the fabric in the dye bath, trying to cover all white parts. Do not stir unless asked to do so, as three-colour mixtures can become muddy.

4 If the dye bath or container has a lid, put it on securely. Otherwise put the dye bath in a plastic bag and seal with clothes pegs (pins). Leave undisturbed for 24–48 hours, then remove the fabric and rinse thoroughly until the water is clear.

5 Wash in hot water with a little washing-up liquid added and then rinse again until the water runs clear. Allow fabrics to dry partially, then iron dry and air before using.

Making a solution for use with acid dyes

Acid-dyeing produces much more colourfast colours in silk than reactive dyeing. The dye is held in the fabric with acid – a vinegar. Make sure that the pans you use will not corrode.

Acid dyes will work only with the addition of an acid (such as white vinegar) to the dye bath. They are available as powder, which must be dissolved in boiling water, or in liquid form. They can be used on wool, alpaca, angora, cashmere and silk, but not on cotton or linen. The resulting colours are light-fast and will not bleach with washing. Always use a metal dye bath when working with acid dyes.

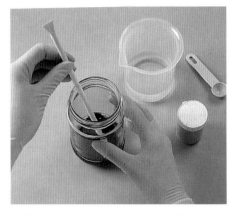

1 To make up a stock acid dye solution, pour 300ml/½ pint water into a jar, mark the level and pour it away. Measure 2.5ml/½ tsp dye powder into the jar and stir to a paste with a little cold water.

2 Add boiling water while stirring until the 300ml/½ pint mark is reached. This mixture will remain stable for several months.

Space-dyeing wool with acid dyes

Acid dyes work just as well on wool as they do on silk, and are excellent for dyeing knitting wool in hanks.

1 Weigh the material to be dyed. Soak it in warm water with a little washing-up (dishwashing) liquid added for at least 30 minutes. Squeeze out excess water gently, without wringing or rubbing. Crumple fabrics and place in the bottom of a metal pan, but lay skeins of yarn so that a maximum amount of the surface area is showing.

2 For each colour to be used, measure the volume of stock dye solution and pour it into a measuring beaker. Add any water necessary to make it up to the volume required. Pour the dyes carefully over the wool, aiming to cover all the white parts, and leave for 10 minutes. Use a maximum of 1½–2 times the volume of dye to fabric and yarn.

3 Add 1–3 times the volume of vinegar to fabric (more for deep colours) to water and pour in the side of the bath. Bring slowly to the boil. The dye should stay on the yarn: if the liquid is not clear, add vinegar. Simmer for 30 minutes. Remove from the heat and allow to cool. Rinse in hot water, adding cold water to cool the wool gradually. Squeeze out and dry.

Space-dyeing silk with acid dyes

Silk can be coloured with a glorious array of brightly coloured tones, muted shades and random patterns when dyed with acid dyes.

Acid-dyeing produces much faster colours in silk than reactive dyeing. The dye bath is heated to fix the dyes, but the silk must not boil or it will harden and crease badly. Using a water bath may make it easier to control the temperature.

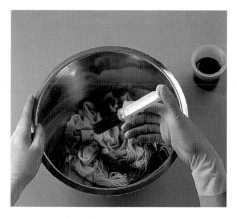

1 Weigh the silk then soak in warm water with a little washing-up (dishwashing) liquid added for at least 30 minutes. Squeeze out excess water and place fabric or yarn in the bottom of a metal pan.

2 For each colour to be used, measure the volume of stock dye solution and pour it into a measuring beaker. Add any water necessary to make it up to the volume required. Refer to the specific recipe.

3 Pour the dyes carefully over the silk. The total volume of dye should not be more than 1½–2 times the weight of the fabric or yarn: a larger amount may be used, but a flatter, more even colour will result.

4 Dye tends to colour silk quite fast, so make sure that all the white parts are covered. Leave for 10 minutes.

5 Use 1–3 times the volume of white vinegar to fabric, using more for deeper colours. Add the white vinegar to water and pour down the side of the dye bath so that it barely covers the fabric or yarn.

6 Heat the dye bath slowly to no more than 85°C/185°F, using a thermometer to check the temperature constantly. After 30 minutes at this temperature, remove from the heat and allow to cool before rinsing.

Fabric painting with reactive dyes

This permanent method of painting fabric can be used for many natural fabric types. Experiment with different painting tools.

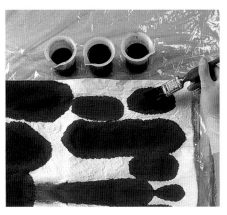

1 Make 300ml/½ pint soda solution up to 1.5 litres/2¾ pints with water and immerse the prepared dry fabric for 10 minutes. Remove and allow to dry. Make up a solution of chemical water by dissolving 120g/4oz urea in 1 litre/1¾ pints hot water.

2 Measure 2.5ml/½ tsp dye into a small beaker. Add a few drops of cold water and stir to a paste. Add the chemical water slowly while stirring to make up the volume to 100ml/ 3½fl oz. Repeat for each colour used.

3 Arrange the fabric on a large plastic sheet to protect the work surface. Paint on the first colour with large brush strokes, evenly spaced over the surface. Wash the brush clean in cold water and allow to dry before changing colours.

4 Paint the subsequent colours evenly in the spaces, allowing some overlapping of the dye solutions. A smaller brush will give a more delicate effect and the dye solutions can be made up weaker if required.

5 Place a second sheet of plastic over the fabric and roll up around a length of plastic piping. Additional pieces of fabric can be rolled on top.

6 Put the roll inside another plastic bag and seal. Leave for 24–48 hours. Remove the fabric and rinse in cold water until it runs clear. Wash in hot soapy water and rinse again. Allow to dry partially, then iron dry.

For a floating summer window dressing, space-dye muslin (cheese-cloth) using the method for pale colours to give pastel shades. Decorate it with machine-stitched lines and tiny beads.

Delicate Muslin Curtain

you will need

curtain-weight muslin (cheesecloth) to fit window, allowing 15cm/6in per drop for hems and casings, plus shrinkage, pre-washed

cold-water reactive dyes, in red, blue, lemon yellow and green

washing soda (sodium carbonate)

dyeing equipment, including rubber gloves, measuring spoons, beakers, glass jars, stirring rods and large plastic tray

iron and thick towel

scissors

multi-coloured machine embroidery thread (floss)

sewing machine

matching sewing thread

fine needle

small pearl and/or glass beads

Recipe for 2.5m/2¾yd of muslin

• 19ml/4 tsp red dye solution + 40ml/1½fl oz soda solution + water to make 250ml/9fl oz

• 19ml/4 tsp blue dye solution + 40ml/1½fl oz soda solution + water to make 250ml/9fl oz

• 8ml/1½ tsp lemon yellow + 12ml/2½ tsp green dye solutions + 40ml/1½fl oz soda solution + water to make 250ml/9fl oz

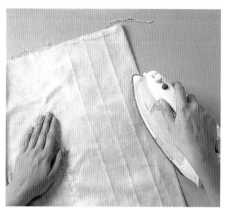

1 Space-dye the muslin, using the cold water reactive method for pale colours described (see Techniques). Use stock dye solutions of 2.5ml/½ tsp dye in 300ml/½ pint hot water. Wash the fabric and iron dry. Trim the side edges, then fold in half lengthways. Working on one-quarter of the curtain at a time, press lengthways folds 3–4cm/1¼–½in apart.

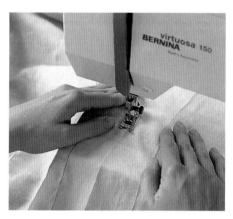

2 Using multi-coloured embroidery thread (floss), machine stitch along the pressed lines. Begin stitching at varying distances from the top and stitch to the bottom of the curtain. Start each row with a few reverse stitches. Cut the bobbin thread at the top, but leave the front thread hanging. Press the curtain.

3 Using matching thread, stitch a 5cm/2in double hem at the base of the curtain, and a 2.5cm/1in casing at the top. Thread a fine needle with the loose thread at the top of each row and attach a bead. Add further beads at random intervals down each row. Press lightly on the wrong side, resting the curtain on a thick towel. Check that the heat of the iron will not melt the beads.

Space-dye an assortment of rich fabrics together, using four shades of dye simultaneously, then assemble them into a traditional Victorian crazy patchwork design.

Crazy Patchwork Cushion

you will need

50cm/½yd white silk-satin, pre-washed

small amounts of textured silks, cotton and viscose fabrics (e.g. taffeta, beaded silk, brocade, cotton velvet)

short lengths of cotton lace

2m/2yd viscose cord

cold water reactive dyes, in blue, black, green and lemon yellow

washing soda (sodium carbonate)

dyeing equipment, including rubber gloves, plastic dye bath, jam jars, stirring rods, measuring beakers, plastic bag and clothes pegs (pins)

iron

ruler

lightweight calico

scissors

pencil

dressmaker's pins

needle

tacking (basting) thread

matching sewing thread

sewing machine

35cm/13½in zipper

40cm/16in square cushion pad

Recipe for 100g/3½oz fabric

• 50ml/2fl oz blue dye solution + 25ml/5 tsp soda solution

• 50ml/2fl oz black dye solution + 25ml/5 tsp soda solution

• 40ml/1½fl oz green + 20ml/4 tsp lemon yellow dye solutions + 30ml/1fl oz soda solution

• 25ml/5 tsp green + 25ml/5 tsp blue dye solutions + 25ml/5 tsp soda solution

1 Weigh the fabrics and adjust the recipe if necessary. Use solutions of 5ml/1 tsp dye in 300ml/½ pint hot water. Space-dye all the fabrics, lace and cord using the cold-water reactive dye method for deep colours.

2 Rinse and wash the dyed fabrics then iron dry. Leave the fabrics to air. Cut two 45cm/18in squares of lightweight calico. Mark the size of the cushion on one square in pencil, adding 2.5cm/1in seam allowance all round. Draw a 5cm/2in border inside the square, on both sides of the calico.

3 Cut a 43cm/17in square of the dyed silk-satin for the back of the cushion, and tack (baste) to the unmarked piece of calico. Trim the calico to size. Cut four strips of dyed silk-satin, each 7.5 x 44cm/3 x 17½in, and reserve for the borders.

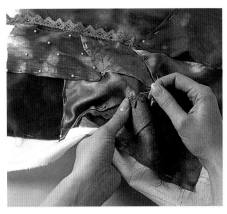

4 Cut pieces of the other dyed fabrics and position them in a random design on the centre square of the cushion front. Press under 5mm/¼in along the edges of the lighter fabrics and overlap them over the heavier fabrics. Overlap each patch by at least 1cm/½in. Pin in place.

5 Insert pieces of lace into some seams, hiding the raw ends under adjacent pieces of fabric. Neatly slip stitch the dyed patches to the calico backing, working from the centre outwards. Ensure that the patches remain flat and that there are no gaps.

6 Pin two of the borders, right sides down, to opposite sides of the patchwork. Stitch along the marked line with a 1cm/½in seam allowance. Press the borders outwards. Repeat with the other two borders. Trim the front to 43cm/17in square. Press under a small hem along one side of the front and the back. Insert the zipper. Pin, then stitch the remaining sides, leaving a 5mm/¼in gap near the zipper. Turn through and press. Slip stitch the dyed cord to the seamline and beside the zip on the front, inserting the knotted ends into the small gap. Slip stitch to close and insert the cushion pad.

These pretty little pyramid-shaped bags are made out of triangles of spray-dyed fabric, decorated with small beads and a ribbon loop for hanging over a coat-hanger.

Spray-dyed Lavender Bags

you will need

reactive dye solutions, in red, blue and violet, made up in chemical water

spray-dyeing equipment, including rubber gloves, spray bottles, measuring beakers and syringes

scraps of loosely-woven white cotton fabrics (e.g. cheesecloth or voile), pre-washed

paper and pencil

scissors

sewing machine

matching sewing thread

narrow ribbon

dried lavender

needle

small pearl beads

1 With your choice of colours spray-dye the fabric (see Techniques). Enlarge the template at the back of the book and cut out, marking the positions a, b, c, d, e and f. Using the template, cut out the fabric for the bags, matching the direction of the grain. One triangle makes one bag.

2 Leaving 5mm/¼in seam allowances throughout, fold point a to point b. Machine stitch down to d. Fold point c to meet point ab then stitch down to e. The fabric should now resemble a pyramid shape.

3 Fold a 10cm/4in length of ribbon into a loop. Pin the ends to align with the raw edges of the fabric at point abc, at the top of the pyramid. Pin and stitch down to point f. Turn the bag right side out.

4 Fill the bag loosely with lavender. Neatly slip stitch the opening closed.

5 Stitch small pearl beads around the base of the pyramid shape, securing the thread every three or four beads with a back stitch.

In this lovely design, inspired by Monet's paintings of water-lilies, it is the embroidery threads that are space-dyed. Two kinds of thread are used to give a textured effect.

Embroidered Pincushion

you will need

20cm/8in square of canvas, 10 threads to 2.5cm/1in

plastic sheet

masking tape

medium artist's paintbrush

fabric paints, in green, sapphire blue and light pink

iron

10g/¼oz white silk 4-ply thread

25cm/10in square of white silk-satin

acid dyes, in bright pinky-red, violet, green and reddish-blue

white vinegar

dyeing equipment, including rubber gloves, metal bowls, measuring spoons, glass jars, stirring rod and thermometer

50g/2oz 4-ply white wool (yarn)

paper and pencil

scissors

dressmaker's pins

felt-tipped pen

ruler

needle

tacking (basting) thread

embroidery needles

25cm/10in square of lightweight calico

sewing machine

matching sewing thread

polyester toy stuffing

thick cardboard

Recipe for the silk thread and silk-satin

• 40ml/1½fl oz dilute pinky-red dye solution

• 20ml/4 tsp dilute violet dye solution

• 40ml/1½fl oz dilute green dye solution

Recipe for 4-ply wool (yarn)

• 5ml/1 tsp reddish-blue dye solution + 60ml/2fl oz water

• 10ml/2 tsp green dye solution + 60ml/2fl oz water

• 5ml/1 tsp violet dye solution + 60ml/2fl oz water

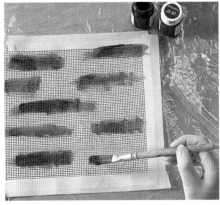

2 Place the canvas on the plastic and secure with tape. Brush green paint evenly over the whole canvas. Add areas of sapphire blue. Cover any remaining areas with pink. Leave to dry for 24 hours. Iron the canvas on the wrong side to fix (set) the dye.

1 Space-dye the silk thread and the silk-satin with acid dyes using your choice of colours, using the method for silk described in Techniques. Use stock solutions of 2.5ml/½ tsp dye in 300ml/½ pint boiling water, diluted by making 20ml/4 tsp dye solution up to 100ml/3½fl oz with water. Iron dry the fabric and hang the thread up to dry.

3 Space-dye 50g/2oz 4-ply wool (yarn) using the method described in Techniques. Use stock solutions of 2.5ml/½ tsp dye in 300ml/½ pint boiling water. Leave to dry thoroughly. Enlarge the template provided to the required size. Cut it out. Pin the paper template to the canvas and draw around it using a felt-tipped pen and ruler. Stitch over the marked lines using tacking (basting) thread.

4 Using two strands of dyed silk thread, fill in the central square of the design area with random long stitch. Work the stitches in varying lengths along each row. Work one row from left to right, then the next row in the opposite direction.

5 Using two strands of wool, work the outer shapes in random long stitch, keeping the top and bottom lines and the diagonal lines as straight edges. Tack the calico to the wrong side of the silk. Pin the silk and canvas right sides together. Stitch around three of the sides into the last row of stitches.

6 Trim the seams, clip the corners and turn through to the right side. Stuff with toy filling (stuffing), then tuck in the seam allowances along the open side. Do not make the pincushion too fat. Neatly slip stitch the opening closed, leaving about 5mm/¼in open at one end.

7 Make a twisted cord from two strands of wool and one of silk. Tie the three ends to a fixed point and twist together. Fold in half, hold the ends and the two lengths will twist together. Knot the two ends together. Tuck the knot into the opening. Couch the cord around the pincushion seam. As you approach the end, re-tie the knot to make it fit exactly and tuck it inside the seam. Stitch the opening.

8 To make the tassels, wind dyed silk around a 4cm/1½in square of cardboard. Push a needle threaded with a length of silk between the pieces of cardboard and knot tightly. Cut the loops at the bottom of the tassel. Double another piece of silk and thread a needle. Wind around the tassel about 1.5cm/⅝in from the top, thread the ends through the loop and pull tight. Stitch into this thread several times to secure. Make four tassels. Trim, then stitch one to each corner.

Painting reactive dyes on to sheer fabric creates a soft, pretty effect even when the colours are vibrant. This practical drawstring bag is lined with waterproof shower fabric.

Dye-painted Cosmetic Bag

you will need

0.5m/½yd cotton lawn or poplin, pre-washed

2m/2yd thick cotton piping cord

cold water reactive dyes, in red, yellow and blue

urea and washing soda (sodium carbonate)

dyeing equipment, including rubber gloves, measuring spoons, beakers and stirring rods

small decorator's paintbrush

plastic sheets, plastic piping, plastic bag and clothes pegs (pins)

small plastic box

iron

tape measure

scissors

50cm/½yd shower curtain fabric

sewing machine

matching sewing thread

dressmaker's pins

needle

tacking (basting) thread

large safety pin

1 Colour the fabric and the piping cord using the painting with reactive dyes method (see Techniques). Put the cord in a small plastic box for 48 hours. Wash the fabric and iron dry.

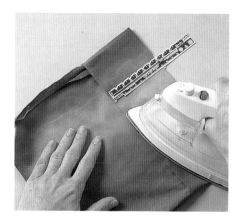

3 Press under 5mm/¼in around the top edge of the bag, then turn down and press a 9cm/3½in hem. Turn the bag right side out.

2 Cut one piece 75 x 27cm/30 x 11in and a piece of shower curtain fabric 55 x 27cm/22 x 11in, for the lining. Fold the lining in half and machine stitch the side seams, leaving a 1cm/½in seam allowance. Fold the dyed fabric in half and stitch both side seams down to 15cm/6in from the top. Leave a 2cm/¾in gap, then stitch to the bottom edge. Press the side seams open.

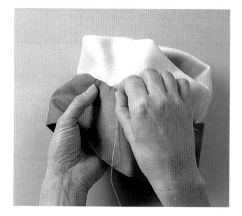

4 Slip the lining inside the bag and tuck it under the hem. Pin the bottom of the hem, then turn the bag inside out and tack (baste) close to the edge. Turn the bag right side out. Using matching thread, machine stitch along the tacking line. To make a casing for the piping, add two more rows of stitching, 7cm/2¾in and 5cm/2in from the top, to correspond with the side seam gaps.

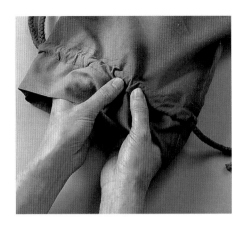

5 Turn the bag inside out and catch the lining to the bag at the lower corners with one or two stitches. Turn the bag right side out and press lightly, ensuring that the heat of the iron does not melt the shower curtain fabric. Cut two lengths of piping cord, each 80cm/32in. Attach a safety pin to one end of one cord and thread through a side opening, around the casing and return to the same opening. Repeat with the second cord through the other opening. Knot the ends of the cord.

Stitch pennant-shaped triangles of vibrant contrast-dyed fabric around this deep blue tablecloth. These instructions are for a cloth 1.40m/55in square, but you can adjust the size to fit your table.

Party Tablecloth

you will need

tape measure

scissors

3.7m/4yd of 1.5m/59in-wide cotton poplin, pre-washed

cold-water reactive dyes in blue, reddish-blue, black, yellow, lemon-yellow, red, violet and green

washing soda (sodium carbonate)

dyeing equipment, including rubber gloves, plastic trays and bags, glass jars, measuring spoons and beakers

iron

paper and pencil

ruler

tailor's chalk

sewing machine

multi-coloured machine embroidery thread (floss)

matching sewing threads

needle

tacking (basting) thread

dressmaker's pins

Recipes

Dark blue

• 540ml/19fl oz blue dye solution + 180ml/6fl oz soda solution

• 540ml/19fl oz reddish-blue dye solution + 180ml/6fl oz soda solution

• 180ml/6fl oz black dye solution + 90ml/3fl oz soda solution

Yellow

• 75ml/2½fl oz yellow dye solution + 40ml/1½fl oz soda solution + 75ml 2½fl oz water

• 75ml/2½fl oz lemon-yellow dye solution + 40ml/1½fl oz soda solution + 75ml/2½fl oz water

Deep pink

• 150ml/5fl oz red dye solution + 70ml/2¼fl oz soda solution

• 75ml/2½fl oz violet dye solution + 40ml/1½fl oz soda solution

Green

• 30ml/1fl oz yellow + 120ml/4fl oz green dye solutions + 75ml/2½fl oz soda solution

• 50ml/2fl oz yellow + 100ml/3½fl oz blue dye solutions + 75ml/2½fl oz soda solution

1 Cut the poplin into four lengths: 2.25m/2½yd for the dark blue tablecloth, bindings and triangles, and three pieces 50cm/20in long for the contrast colours. Space-dye the fabric, using the reactive dye method for deep colours (see Techniques) and stock solutions of 5ml/1 tsp dye in 300ml/½ pint hot water throughout. Fix (set) the colours.

2 Enlarge the triangle template provided to measure 20cm/8in long, plus 1cm/½in seam allowances. Cut 14 triangles in each of the four colours. Cut four strips 5cm x 1.5m/2 x 59in in blue to bind the edge of the cloth.

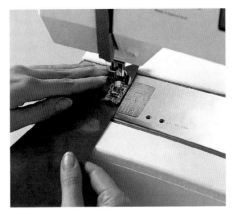

3 Using tailor's chalk, mark a diamond grid on the tablecloth, spacing the lines 20cm/8in apart. Draw the first line diagonally from corner to corner, then work the lines from the centre outwards.

4 Machine stitch along the chalked lines, using multi-coloured machine embroidery thread (floss) and straight stitch. Leaving a 1cm/½in seam allowance and using matching threads, stitch each pair of triangles together along the two bias edges.

5 Trim the corners and turn through, pushing the point of the triangle out, and press. Top stitch close to each edge using multi-coloured thread. Tack (baste) together the unstitched edges of each triangle. There will be seven triangles in each colour.

6 Right sides together, pin and tack the raw edge of the triangles to the edge of the cloth, pointing inwards, lining them up with the stitched grid. Maintain the colour sequence red, yellow, green, blue.

Press under 1cm/½in along one long edge of the bindings. With right sides together and raw edges aligned, pin the binding to two opposite edges of the cloth. Stitch in place.

Press the binding to the wrong side and slip stitch the turned-under edge in place, covering the raw edges of the triangles. Repeat for the other two sides. Top stitch the edge of the tablecloth in a contrast colour.

In this brightly coloured bag, two dyeing methods are used – the pepperpot method of sprinkling dye, and space-dyeing. With each method, dye extra fabric and choose the best pieces for the patchwork.

Patchwork Toy Bag

you will need

1.5m/59in-wide white cotton lawn

2.5m/2¾yd cotton piping cord

cold-water reactive dyes in red, green and violet

salt

washing soda (sodium carbonate)

dyeing equipment, including rubber gloves, plastic trays, measuring beakers, jam jars, plastic bag, clothes pegs (pins), pepperpots (pepper shakers) or muslin squares and household paintbrush

scissors

pencil and ruler

dressmaker's pins

sewing machine

matching sewing threads

iron

large safety pin

Recipe for deep pink

• 400ml/14fl oz red dye solution + 200ml/7fl oz soda solution

1 Space-dye at least four pieces of lawn by the pepperpot (pepper shaker) method using red, green and violet dyes (see Techniques,). Dye 1m/40in lawn and the piping cord deep pink by the reactive space-dyeing method for deep colours (see Techniques). The recipe given is for about 150g/5½oz fabric and cord. Use a stock solution of 5ml/1 tsp dye in 300ml/½ pint hot water. From pepperpot fabric, cut 24 squares, each 12cm/4¾in. From deep pink, cut 24 squares and two pieces 62 x 42cm/24½ x 16½in for the lining.

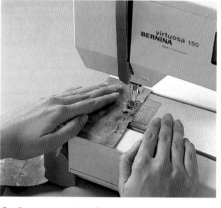

2 Leaving 1cm/½in seams, pin the squares together in rows, alternating the colours. Machine stitch, then press the seams to one side. Make 12 rows of four squares each.

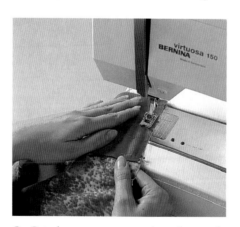

3 Stitch six rows together for each side, alternating the colours. Trim the extra fabric from the corners, then press the seams to one side.

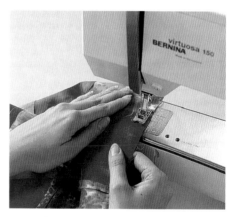

4 Right sides together, pin and stitch both long sides of the lining pieces together, leaving a 1cm/½in seam, to make a tube. Press the seams open. Repeat with the two patchwork pieces, leaving a 3cm/1¼in gap in each side seam 7cm/2¾in from the top. Press the seams open.

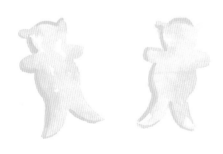

5 With right sides together and side seams matching, slip one tube inside the other. Stitch together around the top, through two layers of fabric. Turn through and press. Top stitch on the outside of the bag. Form the casing for the cord with two rows of machine stitching parallel to the top edge and 7cm/2¾in and 10cm/4in below it.

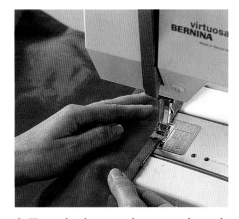

6 Turn the bag inside out and stitch the bottom through all four layers of fabric. Stitch again to reinforce the seam. Trim the bottom edges and tidy with zigzag stitch. Turn through to the right side.

7 Cut the piping cord in half. Attach a safety pin to the end of one piece and thread through a side opening, around the casing and out through the same opening. Repeat with the second piece of cord through the second side opening. Knot all of the ends to finish.

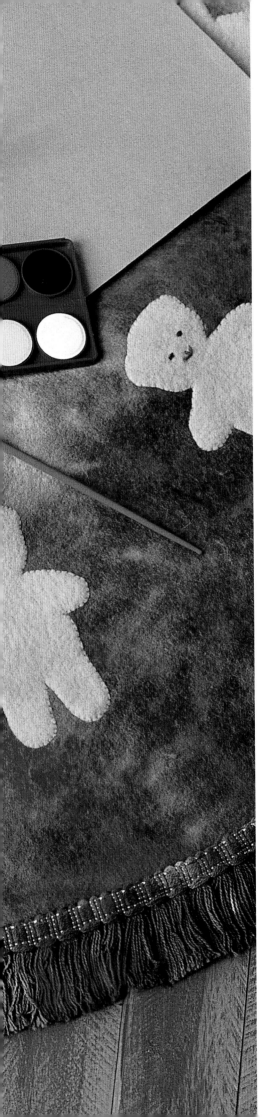

Here colourful space-dyed felt is appliquéd with teddy bears, also in space-dyed felt. The finished rug measures 90cm/36in diameter. Start with a large piece of felt as it could shrink by up to 30 per cent.

Teddy Bear Rug

you will need

1.4m/55in square of wool/viscose felt for the rug, and 50 x 100cm/ 20 x 40in for the teddy bears
cold water reactive dyes, in red, blue, yellow and lemon yellow
washing soda (sodium carbonate)
dyeing equipment, including rubber gloves, large plastic tray, measuring beakers, glass jars and stirring rods
1m/1yd of 1.5m/59in-wide calico
iron
3m/3¼yd white cotton or viscose
fringe or braid
thin paper
tape measure
string
pencil
scissors
heavyweight iron-on interfacing
dressmaker's pins
glue stick
thin cardboard
craft knife and cutting mat
embroidery needle
stranded embroidery thread (floss)
needle
matching sewing thread
fusible bonding web
sewing machine

Recipe for 1.4m/55in square of felt, for the rug 320g/11½oz

• 210ml/7½fl oz red dye solution + 100ml/3½fl oz soda solution + water to make 350ml/12fl oz

• 185ml/6½fl oz blue dye solution + 90ml/3fl oz soda solution + water to make 350ml/12fl oz

• 160ml/5½fl oz yellow dye solution + 90ml/3fl oz soda solution + water to make 350ml/12fl oz

Recipe for 50 x 100cm/20 x 40in, for the bears (70g/2¼oz)

• 100ml/3½fl oz yellow dye solution + 40ml/1½fl oz soda solution

• 100ml/3½fl oz lemon yellow dye solution + 40ml/1½fl oz soda solution

Recipe for 1m/40in of 1.5m/59in-wide calico backing (240g/8½oz)

• 160ml/5½fl oz red dye solution + 75ml/2½fl oz soda solution + water to make 260ml/9½fl oz

• 140ml/4½fl oz blue dye solution + 70ml/2¼fl oz soda solution + water to make 260ml/9½fl oz

• 120ml/4fl oz yellow dye solution + 60ml/2fl oz soda solution + water to make 260ml/9½fl oz

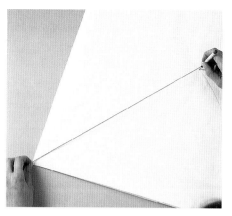

1 Dye the felt for the rug and the teddy bears, using the cold-water reactive space-dyed method for deep colours (see Techniques). Use stock solutions of 2.5ml/½ tsp dye in 300ml/½ pint hot water. After dyeing and washing, the wool/viscose felt can be dried in a tumble drier.

2 Space-dye the calico and bias binding, using the same cold water method for deep colours. Wash and iron dry the calico. Space-dye the fringe or braid, using the same recipe, weighing the dry fringe and adjusting the amount of dye needed. If necessary, reshape the fringe while damp.

3 For the rug pattern, fold a 90cm/36in paper square into quarters. Hold the end of a 45cm/18in length of string in the folded corner, attach the other end to a pencil and draw a quarter circle. Cut out.

4 Using the opened paper pattern, cut out a circle of iron-on interfacing. Pin the interfacing web-side down on to the wrong side of the felt. Fuse the two together, working from the centre out. Cut off the excess felt.

5 Enlarge the teddy template provided, glue it on to cardboard and cut it out. Cut eight yellow felt teddies. Embroider the features.

6 Pin the teddies in a circle, 10cm/4in from the edge of the rug. Slip stitch each teddy to the rug. Iron the back of the rug.

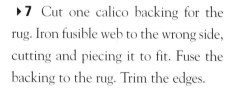

▶**7** Cut one calico backing for the rug. Iron fusible web to the wrong side, cutting and piecing it to fit. Fuse the backing to the rug. Trim the edges.

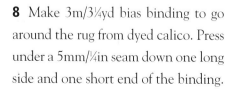

8 Make 3m/3¼yd bias binding to go around the rug from dyed calico. Press under a 5mm/¼in seam down one long side and one short end of the binding.

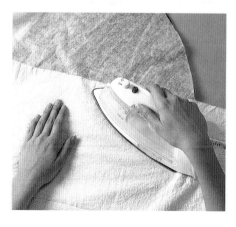

9 Right sides together and raw edges aligned, pin the binding around the rug. Stitch, using a 1cm/½in seam allowance. Overlap the ends by 1cm/½in. Fold the binding over the rug edge and slip stitch it in place on the back. Press flat. On the front, slip stitch the fringe in place over the binding, folding under the raw ends.

Triangular flags, encrusted with beading and embroidery, and finished with tassels, form a distinctive window dressing. Team up with plain curtains dyed to match or use it alone to decorate a small window.

Paisley Pelmet

you will need

50cm/½yd of white cotton poplin

cold-water reactive dyes in yellow and lemon-yellow

washing soda (sodium carbonate)

dyeing equipment, including rubber gloves, plastic trays, glass jars, measuring beakers and syringes

small pieces of silk and cotton textured fabrics

tape measure

scissors

pencil and ruler

bonding powder and fusible web

unwoven pelmet stiffener

dressmaker's pins

baking paper (parchment paper)

iron

glue stick

thin and stiff cardboard

craft knife, rotary cutter and cutting mat

sewing machine

machine embroidery threads (floss), in shades of yellow and gold

embroidery and beading needles

yellow hand embroidery threads (floss), including gold thread

yellow and gold beads

shisha glass (optional)

matching sewing thread

length of 30 x 8mm/1¼ x ⅜in wooden batten, to fit across your window

Yellow recipe for 100g/3½ oz main fabric

• 150ml/5fl oz yellow dye solution + 60ml/2fl oz soda solution

• 150ml/5fl oz lemon-yellow dye solution + 60ml/2fl oz soda solution

Golden yellow recipe for 30g/1oz mixed fabrics

• 120ml/4fl oz yellow dye solution + 60ml/2fl oz soda solution

Lemon yellow recipe for 30g/1oz mixed fabrics

• 100ml/3½ fl oz yellow dye solution + 60ml/2fl oz soda solution

1 Space-dye the poplin yellow using the cold water reactive dye method for deep colours (see Techniques). Use stock solutions of 2.5ml/½ tsp dye in 300ml/½ pint hot water. Dye small pieces of textured fabrics in two other shades of yellow.

2 Cut the batten casing from yellow poplin, 20cm/8in wide and as long as the batten, plus 3cm/1¼in all round for turnings. Set aside. Mark out a piece 10cm/4in wide and as long as the batten for the front of the batten, and as many 12 x 20cm/4¾ x 8in right-angled triangles as will fit across the window.

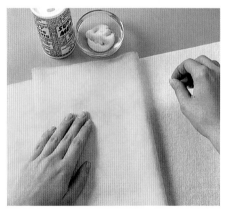

3 Bond the fabric for the flags and casing strip front to the pelmet stiffener using bonding powder. Sprinkle the powder over the stiffener, pin the poplin over the top and cover with baking paper (parchment paper) to protect the iron. Use a warm iron to bond the fabrics. Leave to cool.

4 Iron fusible bonding web to the wrong side of small pieces of the textured fabrics. Enlarge the paisley template from the back of the book to 4cm/1½in long. Glue on to thin cardboard and cut out using a craft knife or rotary cutter. Draw around the template on to the paper backing and cut out the fabric shapes.

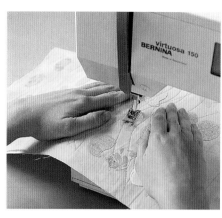

5 Bond the shapes to the flags and central 3cm/1¼in of the casing strip, avoiding the pencil outlines. Using machine embroidery threads (floss), stitch gentle curved lines over and around the paisley shapes.

6 Decorate the flags with hand embroidery. Use chain stitch to surround the shapes and cable chain to stitch curvy lines.

7 Cut out the flags and trim the casing strip to 3cm/1¼in wide, using a rotary cutter. Add beads and shisha glass, if desired.

10 To make the tassels, cut two pieces of thick cardboard 7cm/2¾in square. Wind silk thread around the cards until the tassel is fat enough, then push a needle and thread between them at the top and tie tightly.

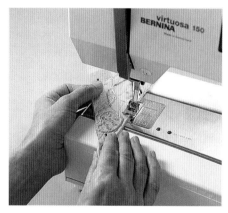

8 Cut an equal number of triangles from spare poplin. Pin each decorated flag to a backing piece then machine stitch around the edge with a small, narrow zigzag stitch.

11 Cut the loops at the bottom between the cards. Wind double thread around each tassel about 1.5cm/⅝in from the top, thread the ends through the loop, pull tight and tie. Trim the bottom. Stitch one tassel to the end of each flag.

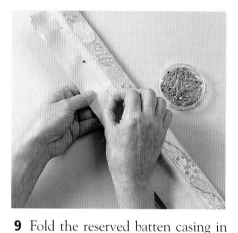

9 Fold the reserved batten casing in half lengthways and press. Turn under and press 1.5cm/⅝in at each short end. Pin the decorated casing strip 3mm/⅛in from the foldline and stitch with a narrow zigzag. Pin the casing loosely around the batten. Remove the batten and stitch along the pinned line. Stitch the flags securely to the casing, just under the previous seam. Press the raw edges of the casing up, insert the batten then slip stitch the raw edges in place.

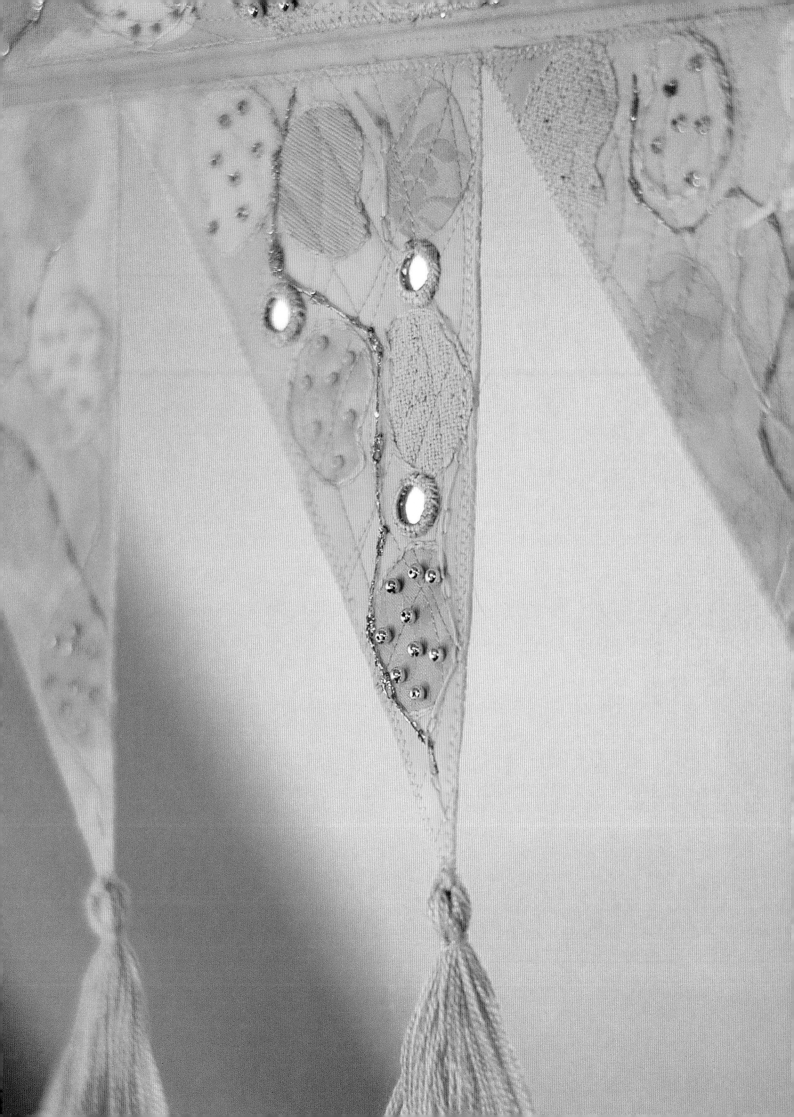

Over a brilliantly coloured patchwork background of space-dyed fabrics, this panel is appliquéd with silk and felt "Indian birds" and completed with decorative hand stitching in acid-dyed silk.

Quilted Wallhanging

you will need

1m/40in calico or white cotton fabric, 1.5m/60in wide, plus lightweight calico for backing and batten sleeve

tape measure

scissors

cold-water reactive dyes in red, yellow, lemon, lemon, blue, reddish-blue, green

washing soda (sodium carbonate)

dyeing equipment, including rubber gloves, plastic bowls, trays, measuring beakers and syringes

iron

cutting mat

ruler

rotary cutter

pins

sewing machine

matching sewing thread

felt interlining

tacking (basting) thread

needle

acid-dyed silk embroidery thread (floss)

four birds and one flower using the techniques shown in the Indian Birds project

44cm/17¾in batten

"D" moulding curtain rings

Recipes

Pink

• 10ml/2 tsp red dye solution + 30ml/1fl oz soda solution + water to make 160ml/5½fl oz

Pale yellow – pour each made-up solution on separately

• 10ml/2 tsp yellow dye solution + 20ml/4 tsp soda solution + water to make 80ml/2¾fl oz

• 10ml/2 tsp lemon dye solution + 20ml/4 tsp soda solution + water to make 80ml/2¾fl oz

Pale blue – pour each made-up solution on separately

• 10ml/2 tsp blue dye solution + 20ml/4 tsp soda solution + water to make 80ml/2¾fl oz

• 10ml/2 tsp reddish-blue dye solution + 20ml/4 tsp soda solution + water to make 80ml/2¾fl oz

Pale green

• 10ml/2 tsp green dye solution + 10ml/2 tsp lemon dye solution + 30ml/1fl oz soda solution + water to make 160ml/5½fl oz

Mid-green

• 85ml/3fl oz lemon yellow dye solution + 170ml/6fl oz green dye solution + 80ml/2¾fl oz soda solution

1 Cut the calico for the hanging into four squares each 50cm/20in, and one rectangle 50 x 100cm/20 x 40in. Space-dye each square (each should weigh about 45g/1¼ oz) a different colour for the centre triangles. Use the cold-water reactive space-dyed method for pale colours described in the Techniques section. The stock solutions are 2.5ml/½ tsp dye in 300ml/½ pint hot water. Dye the rectangle mid-green using the cold-water space-dyed method for deep colours and the same strength stock solutions. Leave to dry and iron flat.

2 Cut a 20cm/8in square of each pale colour. Cut each square diagonally into four triangles. Arrange the triangles to form the pattern shown. Pin and stitch the yellow and blue triangles together with a 1cm/½in seam. Press the seam towards the darker colour.

3 Pin and stitch the pink and green triangles together. Keeping the triangle arrangement correct, sew the pink/green triangles to the blue/yellow triangles with a 1cm/½in seam to form four squares. Press on the wrong side.

4 Cut strips 7cm/2¾ in wide for the border from mid-green calico. From the 7cm/2¾in-wide strips, cut two strips each 17cm/6½in long, cut three strips 37cm/14½in long, and two strips 47cm/18½in long.

5 With a 1cm/½in seam allowance throughout, stitch one side of each square to one side of each 17cm/6½in strip. Press the seams towards the middle. Between the two panels, stitch a 37cm/14½in strip. Press the square flat.

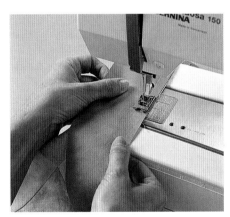

6 Stitch 37cm/14½in strips to the top and bottom of the patchwork. Attach the long strips down each side. Check that the patchwork is square and trim if necessary.

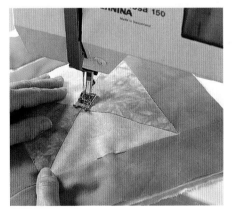

7 To make the backing, cut one 47cm/18½in square from lightweight calico and one from felt interlining. Sandwich the interlining between the backing and the patchwork. Pin together from the centre outwards. Quilt using toning thread and stitching along the seamlines, working from the centre outwards. Tack (baste) the edges and trim.

8 For the edging, cut a 17 x 20cm/ 6½ x 8in piece of each pale fabric. Join the long sides in the colour order yellow, pink, green and blue. Press the seams to one side, then cut across them to make four strips 4cm/1½in wide. Accurately press under 0.5cm/¼in along one long edge of each strip.

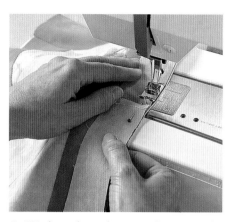

9 With right sides together, match the pink/green seam on the unpressed edge of a length of binding to the centre top of the patchwork. Pin and stitch with a 1cm/½in seam allowance. Press the seam. Repeat at the bottom edge.

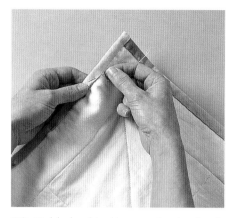

10 Fold the binding to the back of the quilt and neatly slipstitch the folded edge in place. Repeat for the bottom edge, then add the sides in the same way. Turn in the raw edges of each short end to align with the quilt edge. Press and neatly stitch the ends in place.

11 Using acid-dyed silk embroidery threads (floss), work a row of decorative running stitch around the inside edge of each triangle. Work several parallel rows along the border. Make up four different-coloured Indian birds, following the instructions in the Indian Birds project.

12 Pin and stitch a silk and felt bird in the centre of each square. Make a green flower to match the birds using the template at the back of the book. Enlarge the flower to 17cm/6½in wide, and make up in the same way as the Indian birds. Stitch it in place on the quilt centre.

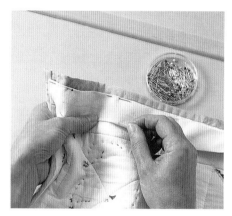

13 To make a batten sleeve, cut a strip of undyed calico 7.5 x 46cm/3 x 18in and press under 1cm/½in at each short end. Fold in half lengthways and stitch with a 1cm/½in seam. Press the seam open at the back of the tube. Slipstitch in place on the back of the hanging. Insert the batten into the sleeve and stitch on curtain rings for hanging.

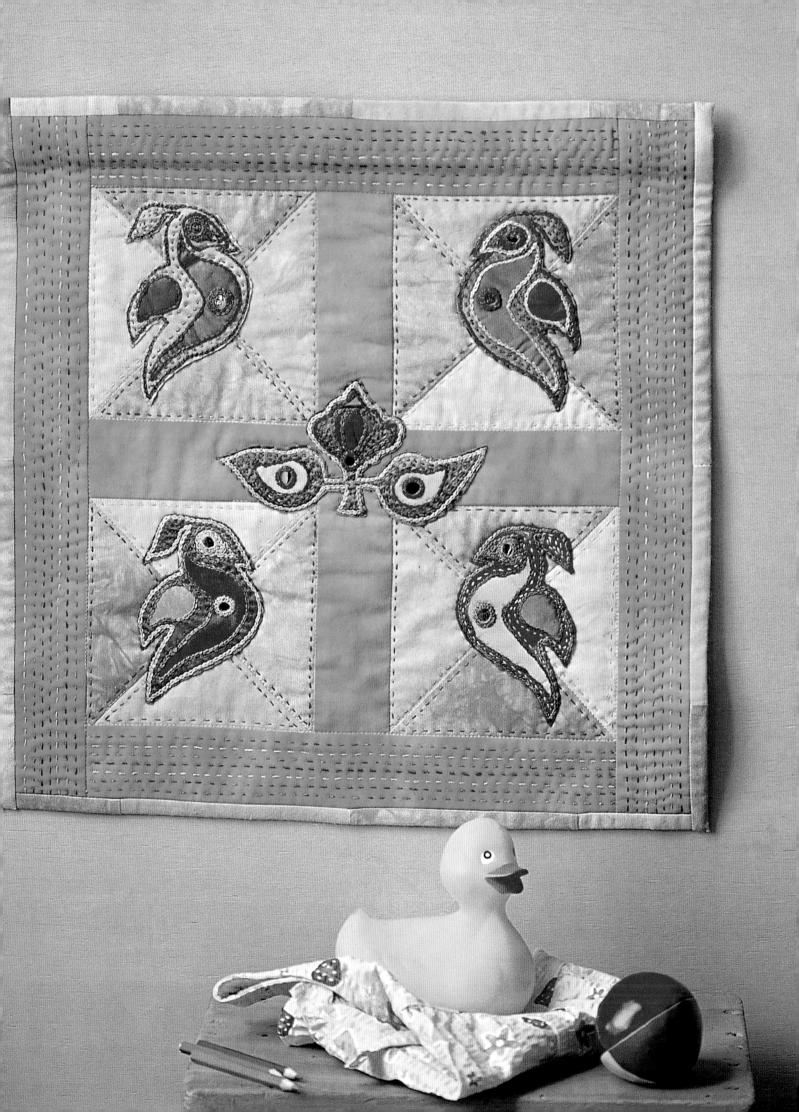

These vibrant birds are made from silk satin and dyed felt, sandwiched together and embellished with embroidery and shisha glass. They can be used as appliquéd decorations or stuffed to make ornaments.

Indian Birds

you will need

100 x 56cm/40 x 22in silk satin

silk thread

acid dyes for silk: pink, mid-red, yellow, lemon, blue and red-blue

vinegar

dyeing equipment including rubber gloves, plastic trays, metal pans, beakers, syringes and stirring rods

4 x 20in squares wool/viscose felt

cold-water reactive dyes for viscose: red, yellow, lemon, green, blue and red-blue

washing soda (sodium carbonate)

iron

scissors

bonding powder and/or fusible web

baking parchment

thin cardboard, glue stick, craft knife and cutting mat

pencil

sewing machine

needle

shisha glass

polyester toy filling (stuffing)

Blue felt (reactive dye)

• 50ml/2fl oz blue dye solution + 30ml/1fl oz soda solution + water to make 100ml/3½fl oz

• 50ml/2fl oz red/blue dye solution + 30ml/1fl oz soda solution + water to make 100ml/3½fl oz

Recipes

Blue silk (acid dye)

• 80ml/2¾fl oz stock red-blue

• 30ml/1fl oz stock blue

Red silk (acid dye)

• 110ml/3¾fl oz stock pink/red

• 40ml/1½fl oz stock mid-red

Red felt (reactive dye)

• 10ml/2 tsp red dye solution + 30ml/1fl oz soda solution + water to make 200ml/7fl oz

Yellow silk (acid dye)

• 35ml/1¼fl oz stock yellow

• 35ml/1¼fl oz stock lemon

Yellow felt (reactive dye)

• 50ml/2fl oz yellow dye solution + 30ml/1fl oz soda solution + water to make 100ml/3½fl oz

• 50ml/2fl oz lemon dye solution + 30ml/1fl oz soda solution + water to make 100ml/3½fl oz

Green silk (acid dye)

• 85ml/3fl oz stock lemon dye solution + 70ml/2¼fl oz stock blue dye solution

Green felt (reactive dye)

• 80ml/2¾fl oz green + 20ml/4 tsp yellow dye solution + 50ml/2fl oz soda solution + water to make 200ml/7fl oz

1 Space-dye the silk satin and silk thread with acid dyes using the method described in the Techniques section. Each recipe makes enough dye for 32g/1¼oz, which includes 20g/¾oz fine silk thread and a piece of silk satin 25 x 56cm/10 x 22in. Add about 200ml/7fl oz vinegar to the water. All stock solutions are made using 2.5ml/½ tsp dye in 300ml/½ pint boiling water.

2 Space-dye felt in colours to match the silk using cold-water reactive dyes for deep colours as described in the Techniques section. The recipes use stock solutions of 2.5ml/½ tsp dye in 300ml/½ pint hot water and will each dye a piece of felt about 50cm/20in square (about 35g/1¼oz). Allow the fabric to dry thoroughly after ironing.

3 Cut a piece of silk large enough to make two or three birds and a piece of felt the same size. Fuse the silk on top of the felt with bonding powder by pressing with a hot iron, protecting the iron with baking parchment. Repeat for all four colours.

4 Enlarge the template to 12.5cm/ 5in. Glue the copy on to cardboard and cut out. Draw around the template on the felt side of the bonded fabrics, turning it over to produce mirror images for half the birds. Stab stitch or machine embroider the outline, following the pencil line.

5 To add contrasting panels on the bird's body and wing, bond fusible web to the wrong side of various colours of silk. Draw around the templates on to the paper side of the webbing and accurately cut out each shape. Peel off the paper and pin each shape in place.

6 Iron contrasting colour shapes on the background. Chain stitch around the outline of each bird, the wing and head. Add rows of running stitch and decorative shisha glass if you like. Chain stitch the eye. When the embroidery is complete, cut around the shape. At this stage, the birds can be applied to the Quilted Wallhanging. For a hanging bird, make a short cord from thread. Form a loop and stitch the ends behind the top of the bird's head. Oversew a pair of mirror-image birds together. Stuff softly with toy filling (stuffing) before the stitching is complete.

Templates

Enlarge the templates on a photocopier. Alternatively, trace the design and draw a grid of evenly spaced squares over your tracing. Draw a larger grid on to another piece of paper and copy the outline square by square. Finally, draw over the lines to make sure they are continuous.

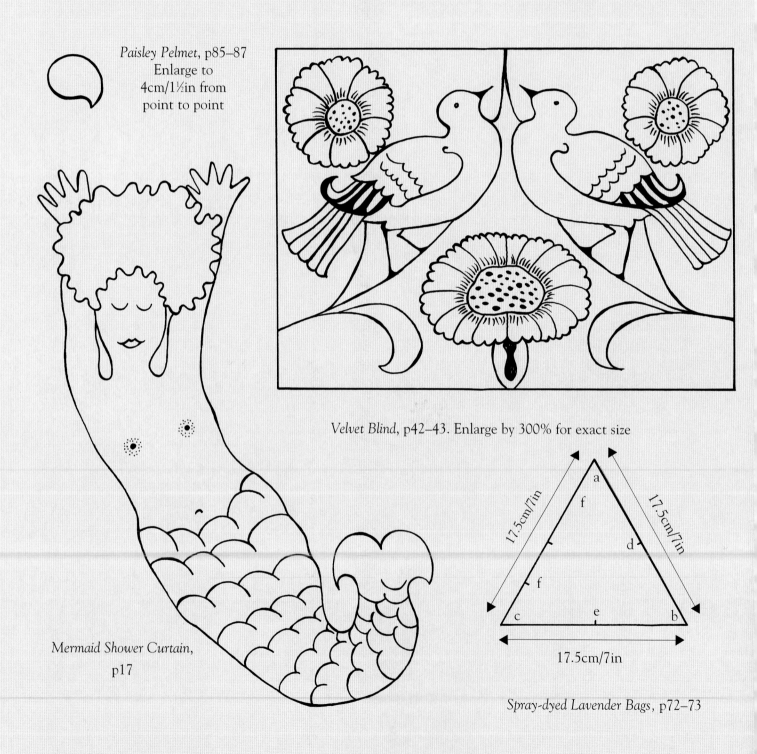

Paisley Pelmet, p85–87
Enlarge to
4cm/1½in from
point to point

Velvet Blind, p42–43. Enlarge by 300% for exact size

Mermaid Shower Curtain,
p17

17.5cm/7in
17.5cm/7in
17.5cm/7in

a
f
f
d
c   e   b

Spray-dyed Lavender Bags, p72–73

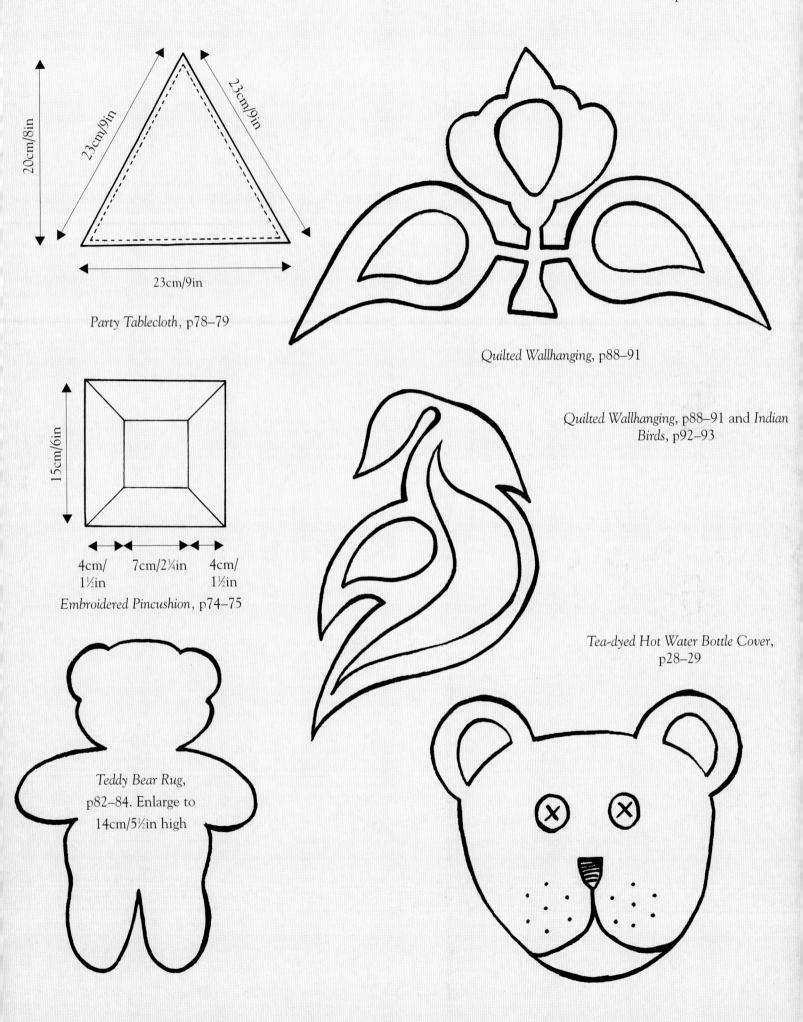

20cm/8in

23cm/9in

23cm/9in

23cm/9in

Party Tablecloth, p78–79

Quilted Wallhanging, p88–91

15cm/6in

4cm/
1½in

7cm/2¾in

4cm/
1½in

Embroidered Pincushion, p74–75

Quilted Wallhanging, p88–91 and Indian Birds, p92–93

Tea-dyed Hot Water Bottle Cover, p28–29

Teddy Bear Rug, p82–84. Enlarge to 14cm/5½in high

Index

acid dyes 65–66

bedspread, tie-dyed patchwork 52–53
birds, Indian space-dyed 92–93, 95
blind, velvet 42–43, 94
bonding powder 60
book cover, marbled 54–55

cold-water dyes:
  deep colours 64
  pale colours 63
  preparing 62
cosmetic bag, dye-painted 76–77
crazy patchwork cushion 70–71
curtain, space-dyed 68–69
cushions: dip-dyed floor 44–45
  space-dyed crazy patchwork 70–71
  tie-dyed patchwork 48–49

desk set, marbled 36–37
dip-dyeing 14
  floor cushion 44–45
  lampshades 18–19, 40–41
  place mats 30–31
dishwashing liquid 60
double-dyed place mats 30–31
doughnut floor cushion 44–45
drawstring bag, marbled 22–23
duvet cover, tie-dyed 46–47
dye baths 13
dye-painted cosmetic bag 76–77
dye solution, making up 14
dyeing and marbling 9–11
  equipment 13
  materials 12
  techniques 14–16
dyes 12, 60

embroidered pincushion 74–75

fabric etching medium 12
  velvet blind 42–43, 94

fabrics 12, 60
floor cushion, dip-dyed 44–45
floss see threads
folded napkin parcels 50–51
folded silk handkerchiefs 32–33
fusible web 60

handkerchiefs, folded silk 32–33
headband, marbled 26–27
hot water bottle cover, tea-dyed 28–29, 95

Indian birds 92–93, 95

jewellery roll, tie-dyed 38–39

lampshades: dip-dyed 18–19
  tassel-edged 40–41
lavender bags, spray-dyed 72–73, 94

marbling 16
  book cover 54–55
  desk set 36–37
  drawstring bag 22–23
  headband 26–27
  spectacle case 24–25
marbling thickening medium 12
mermaid shower curtain 17, 94
muslin curtain, space-dyed 68–69

napkins, tie-dyed 50–51
non-woven interfacing 60

painting fabric with reactive dyes 67
  cosmetic bag 76–77
paisley pelmet 85–87, 94

paper 12
party tablecloth 78–79, 95
patchwork bedspread, tie-dyed 52–53
patchwork cushions: space-dyed 70–71
  tie-dyed 48–49
patchwork toy bag 80–81
pelmet, space-dyed paisley 85–87, 94
pepperpot method 62
  patchwork toy bag 80–81
pincushion, embroidered 74–75
place mats, double-dyed 30–31
pleated table runner 34–35

quilted wallhanging 88–91, 95

resist medium 12
rug, space-dyed teddy bear 82–84, 95

shower curtain 17, 94
silk, acid-dyeing 66
sodium carbonate 60, 62
space-dyeing 57–59
  embroidered pincushion 74–75
  equipment 61
  Indian birds 92–93, 95
  materials 60
  muslin curtain 68–69
  paisley pelmet 85–87, 94
  party tablecloth 78–79
  patchwork cushion 70–71
  patchwork toy bag 80–81
  quilted wallhanging 88–91, 95
  techniques 62–67
  teddy bear rug 82–84, 95

spectacle case, marbled 24–25
spray-dyeing 63
  lavender bags 72–73, 94

tablecloth, space-dyed 78–79, 95
table runner, pleated 34–35
tassel-edged lampshade 40–41
tea-dyed hot water bottle cover 28–29, 95
teddy bear rug 82–84, 95
templates 94–95
threads, dyeing 60
  embroidered pincushion 74–75
  Indian birds 92–93, 95
  quilted wallhanging 88–91, 95
throw, velvet-edged 20–21
tie-dyeing 15
  duvet cover 46–47
  jewellery roll 38–39
  napkins 50–51
  patchwork bedspread 52–53
  patchwork cushion 48–49
  silk handkerchiefs 32–33
  table runner 34–35
toy bag, patchwork 80–81

urea 60

vanishing fabric marker 13
velvet blind 42–43, 94
velvet-edged throw 20–21

wallhanging, quilted 88–91, 95
washing soda 60, 62
washing-up liquid 60
wool, acid-dyeing 65